MAL MAR
TREE FARM

MAL MAR PROPERTY
MANAGEMENT

MAL MAR
TREE CONES

POWER
PETROLEUM INC.

...ND IT CAME TO PASS...

DAVE MALLORY
WITH
TOM MARX

ISBN: 1467919454
ISBN 13: 9781467919456

Library of Congress Control Number: 2011961710
CreateSpace, North Charleston, SC

This book is dedicated to the Pizzagalli brothers, Angelo, Remo, and Jim, who did so much to help Tom and I be as successful as we were. You guys were great! Thank you, thank you!

Many thanks again to my wonderful wife, Pauline, who is able to make sense out of my ideas, to Bob Hinkley who edits and gives me logical choices on how to say things, to Doreen Malnati who takes my wild ideas and magically creates a cover, and to my nephew, Jeff Fountain, who set up the Dragon Speak program and spent many hours putting everything into Microsoft Word. This book would not happen without the four of you.

And many, many thanks to my loyal and faithful business partner, Tom Marx, who took the time and energy to develop my business sense and be so successful with him.

And It Came To Pass

This is the story of two guys from different backgrounds, one German, the other Irish, separated by distance and age. They met in a church choir, one age 16, the other age 8, and over a period of years formed a very good friendship and went into business. They developed and ran four businesses over a period of 26 years, worked hard, saved their money, invested wisely, and retired early to Florida with no debt and many large assets. How did it happen? Read their story.

Part I

The Early Years

It was 1966. We were at a party at Pine Haven Shore, a common occurrence. Pine Haven was in Shelburne, Vermont and it was Tom's mother's home. We were in the yard looking out over Lake Champlain having a beer, another common occurrence. It was Tom's 32nd birthday. He said to me, "Do you have any money?" Fortunately I had parents and a grandfather who taught me how to save. I said, "Yes, I'm 24 and I have $2200 in the bank." Tom asked me what I was going to do with it. I said, "I'm going to buy a used Porsche." He said, "No you aren't. We are going out to look for some land instead, because it is a good investment." And that, dear readers, was the beginning of a very successful business partnership.

Tom's Mother's Home at Pine Haven Shore

CHAPTER 1

"The only thing we have to fear is fear itself."

F. D. ROOSEVELT

The first half of this partnership was born in Westbury, Long Island, New York, in 1934, to Dr. Frank and Peggy Marx. Tom was the youngest of four, having two brothers and one sister. Dr. Marx passed away when Tom was four. Long Island continued to be their home until the start of World War II. At this time the Germans were landing spies from submarines along the coast of New York. Peggy worried about her young family. As the world moved closer to a major war she began to fear the Germans and was sure they would bomb New York. After thinking about what to do, she gathered up her family and moved to Burlington, Vermont. Nobody would bomb Burlington; there were more cows than there were people.

Tom went to Christ the King School and flourished. In 1942 Peggy married Carlton Ryan, an officer in the 187th Field Artillery stationed at Fort Ethan Allen in Essex Junction, Vermont. After the war Carlton and Peggy opened a fabric store called Pegton's Yardstick. In 1951 after their divorce, Peggy built a home at Pine Haven Shore on Shelburne Bay which would be their home in Vermont for many years. That was the site of our first business conversation when Tom told me we're going to go out and look for some land.

In 1942 the stork dropped a bundle of joy to Frank and Gladys Mallory, that would be me. We lived in Burlington on the upper floor of a home owned by my mother's parents. Dad was working as a meat cutter at the Grand Union and mom worked for the George Little Press. After I was born mom quit her job to take care of me. I guess she thought it would be a full-time job. Dad was in the Vermont National Guard and his commander, Dr. Fred

Kent, offered him a job at the University of Vermont to develop a medical photography department at $13 a week! Since I wasn't at the age to offer advice, dad took the job. Although we struggled for a number of years, it turned out to be a good move. He built the department and ran it until he retired in 1978.

Mom and dad decided I needed company and produced a sister in 1947. In 1950 we moved from the south side of Burlington to the north side. We bought one side of a duplex and mom's sister and her family bought the other side from mom's father. I transferred from Christ the King School to Cathedral Grammar School.

It was about this time that things started to get interesting. Tom was attending Cathedral High School and was a member of the choir at Cathedral of the Immaculate Conception Catholic Church. I was in the third grade at Cathedral Grammar School and was also a member of the same choir singing soprano. Although we didn't know it at the time, this was to be the first of many occasions when we would get together. I'm quite sure Tom doesn't remember much of me, an eight-year-old singing soprano, but I remember many of the big guys singing bass and tenor: Tom, Ray Shepherd, Connie Flynn, and Fred Blaise.

Dr. Joseph Lechnyr was born in Prague, Czechoslovakia, in 1896, the son of an army bandmaster. He was very famous throughout the northeast and Canada. He was famous in Vermont as a choir and band director. He was a very strict disciplinarian and would not hesitate to throw his hymnal at you if you didn't pay attention. Needless to say, we paid attention! Dr. Lechnyr was also famous for rewriting "Cotton Babes", the University of Vermont Winter Carnival theme song, after it had been destroyed by fire. This was the oldest Winter Carnival in the country and featured a "Kake Walk" contest by all the fraternities while "walking fo da kake." Unfortunately, "Kake Walk" was stopped by a few people who thought it was making fun of the blacks, but actually it was started by the blacks to make fun of the white people and the funny way they danced. It was too bad to have a few unknowing people have that much influence at a university. In 1957 Dr. Lechnyr stopped a riot at a University of Vermont football game by having the band play the national anthem.

CHAPTER 2

"As long as there are guns, the individual that wants a gun for a crime is going to have one."

Ronald Reagan

Burlington, Vermont was a small New England city of about 25,000 people in the 1950s. The police department was located on Church Street in a two bay, three story building. The two patrol cars were kept inside when not on duty along with the detective car, the ambulance, and two motorcycles. The building had a pistol range in the basement and the office was on the second floor.

The police department was short of officers so Dad approached Chief Don Russell about starting an auxiliary police force. The chief liked the idea so Dad got together with Sterling Emerson and they formed a small auxiliary unit. They were able to raise money for uniforms and were given some surplus World War II equipment, such as Sam Browne belts and pistols. Tom heard about the force and asked Dad if he could join. He was only 18 at the time but Dad said yes he could, but with limited duties. He started working on the force and was stationed on Church Street walking a beat or directing traffic. He would often stop by the house to meet with Dad and that is how we reconnected.

I had joined the Burlington Rifle Club which was run by Ed Keenan, who would become mayor of Burlington from 1963 to 1965. John Barr, who would become a good friend and the Vermont National Guard Chief of Staff, gave us a test which I passed, which made me eligible to shoot. I would walk to the range by way of Church Street on Friday nights and say hello to Dad and Tom. Many times I would be carrying my .22 rifle with me as I walked down Church Street. Boy how times have changed!

As the years went by, the future business partners were busy doing their own thing. Tom was at the University of Vermont in the ROTC program. Upon graduation in 1956 he was assigned to Fort Bliss, Texas, as a second lieutenant in missile defense. I think in those days the missiles consisted of somebody running out, lighting a fuse, and then running away as it took off! After a tour at Fairchild Air Force Base, a Nike missile and Strategic Air Command (SAC) base near Spokane, Washington, Tom went to finance school at Fort Benjamin Harrison. The skills he developed there would be very helpful in business later on. He finally finished his Army career at Camp Irwin, California.

In 1956 I finished Cathedral Grammar School and moved to Cathedral High School. I had switched from playing piano to playing trumpet in the sixth grade, which turned out to be a wise move. I was in the high school band and also the University of Vermont band because Dr. Lechnyr directed both bands. I sang in the chorus and was on the rifle team. In my sophomore year I was elected to vice president of the class with Joe St. George as the president. I was still in the Burlington Rifle Club where I earned the National Rifle Association Junior Distinguished Rifleman Award.

In 1959 Cathedral High School was bursting at the seams. The Catholics were breeding faster than the high school could educate them. Finally, in February, on a cold winter day the student body of about 225 students, along with the staff and faculty, abandoned the three buildings that were the Cathedral High School and marched the 3 miles to Rice Memorial High School in South Burlington. The students followed the band which played marches all the way through the front door of the new school. That was a very exciting day!

Meanwhile, Tom had moved back to Burlington and was working at his mother's shop trying to learn the business. He was doing some of the buying for his mother while looking for a real job! In September we met again. This time I was hitch-hiking a ride home from Rice High School and Tom picked me up on Shelburne Road in his 1955 Thunderbird - the first one in Vermont.

After graduating from Rice High School in 1960, I went to the University of Vermont as a pre-med student. However, after two years of nothing but science classes, I switched my major to business and learned the tools of the trade which would help me later on with our businesses.

6

CHAPTER 3

Winter either bites with its teeth or lashes with its tail

PROVERB

188 Cliff Street Burlington, Vermont

Winters in Vermont can be long and tiring. Throughout all of Vermont's history there has been no month where snow has not fallen. Tom thought Palm Beach, Florida, would have nicer winter weather. He and Peggy had bought a nine-apartment building at 188 Cliff Street in Burlington and shortly after, Peggy sold her inventory and turned her dress shop into four apartments. It was about this time Tom realized just how talented I was! Since he would be spending his winters in Florida while I would be spending my winters in Vermont going to school, he thought that I would be a good property manager. And how right he was, as I had some very unique experiences. My first winter was a squirrel bonus at 188 Cliff Street. Two different pest-control

7

companies were hired to trap the squirrels and dispose of them. Well, the pest-control people left, but not the squirrels. The third guy I hired came highly recommended and he said the squirrels were in between the partitions on the second floor. He said he could poison them but if they didn't leave for water, they would die between the walls and smell the whole building up. I chose to use the poison, and since they left the house with an upset stomach and never returned, I made a lot of points.

The next month I had to evict a prominent Burlington businessman who was having wild parties in his apartment. That was fun. The businessman did not appreciate it, but he finally left. A few weeks later, the fire department was called to put out a fire in the frying pan of General Bilodeau's mother. She had fallen asleep and smoke went all through the building. The Church Street apartments were quiet compared to Cliff Street. Two guys moved in and asked if they could paint the apartment. I told them to go ahead but I wanted to inspect it when they were done. Two weeks later they had me over to inspect. I couldn't believe they painted it a lime green and pink! I decided that my inspection would be quite quick!

In the meantime, Tom became a chauffeur for King Saud of Saudi Arabia for a few weeks. After that he went to work as a personal secretary for Nina (Puddin') Dodge, the heiress to Maxwell House Coffee.

"Puddin" Dodge and Peggy (Tom's Mother)

Hank, Tony, Jeff Dodge and Dave Mallory with Atlantic Sailfish

CHAPTER 4

"Rich Palm Beach clients all wanted
the same kind of different thing."

BILLY BALDWIN

Palm Beach, Florida, was a well-to-do city of about 6500 people in the early 1960s. It was the home of the rich and famous. People like the Kennedys, the Vanderbilts, and many others were often seen in Palm Beach. Puddin' Dodge was in that group and was often featured in the "shiny sheets" of the Palm Beach Post. She was a gorgeous five foot blond with three boys and two girls. Tom went to work for her in 1962 along with Andre the chef, Sarah and Ethel, who helped with the housework, cooking and shopping; and Mam'selle, who took care of the girls.

Tom felt the boys were a quite a challenge and asked me to come help him during my school vacations. Sometimes, in the fall, I would drive a car owned by Henry Riordan to Palm Beach and deliver the car to Henry and his wife when they arrived. Then in the spring I would often drive their car back to Burlington. They would pay for my meals and hotel, and for my flight back home. I always made money when I drove their car because I would never stop between Burlington and Palm Beach. As a result, I never had any hotel expenses and mom would always make sandwiches for me to eat on the road. It was a pretty good deal for me and I always had a lot of fun. Tom bought a guest house on Atlantic Avenue in Palm Beach and sometimes I would stay there, while other times we would stay in the garage apartment at Puddin's house. It always scared the hell out of me to stay at Tom's guest house because of the old woman living next door. She often would come up to me, dressed in nothing but a sheet, and look me in the ear, not my eye, and say, "I have an affinity for you!" I still get the shivers thinking about that one! After the first such experience, Tom informed me her name was "Crazy Mary" and I learned to stay far away from her. However, many times, when she knew I was there, she would wait around outside to see if I was going to come out. I seldom did.

Dave Mallory, Hank and Tony Dodge.
Notice the Bonita head and the Barracuda head

One of my many difficult jobs was to keep the boys busy. One of the things they enjoyed, and their mother liked to see them do, was to go deep sea fishing. Of course they usually had to "twist" my arm but I often relented and we went deep-sea fishing. On one trip I caught a 6 ½ foot Atlantic Sailfish. Puddin' insisted on having it mounted for me. Another time, one of the boys had a Bonita on the line and a big Shark came up and bit it in half.

That same trip I had a big Barracuda on the line and a great big Porpoise came up and bit the Barracuda in half! That was quite a day of fishing. I really had to work hard to keep the boys busy.

Puddin' purchased a home at Pine Haven, so every spring Tom and I would cart some of the family to Vermont and the rest would fly off to Europe. My job during the summers was to entertain the boys - Hank, Tony, and Jeffrey - by taking them out to do things like play miniature golf; going out in Tom's boat; trying to catch turtles in the La Platte River in Shelburne, Vermont; or doing some water skiing. For two summers, I got a "real job" mowing lawns at Shelburne Museum and on weekends I would drive Puddin's old Corvair van to Bridgton, Maine, to visit the boys at Camp Hi Ho Ridge. I would entertain them by taking them on seaplane rides, playing miniature golf, or climbing Pleasant Mountain just outside Bridgton. Some weekends the camp would have a father-son baseball game and I played the part of the father.

Tom would be in Europe for the summer with Puddin', the girls, and the help. His summer job was even better than mine! When Tom returned to Vermont, he would go to Maine with me and we would both play dad. One time we stopped at a motel in New Hampshire on the way to Maine and when we walked into the office, two huge Doberman-pinschers greeted us. One of them jumped on me, put his paws on my shoulders, and looked me right in the eye. That was quite an experience! As we approached the desk, the manager asked Tom, "A room for you and your son?" Tom never forgot that because I never let him forget it.

Chef Andre was a French speaking Canadian with a very quick temper. One time I asked him why there were so many blacks in the United States and so many Frenchmen in Canada. He said he didn't know and asked me why. I said, "Because we had first choice!" He chased Tom and me out of the house with a big butcher knife and chased us around the yard until he finally gave up. He locked the door of the house and kept us out for long time.

That fall we flew Tony, the middle boy, to Exeter Academy in New Hampshire. Tom had gotten his pilot's license when he was in the Army and we thought it would be fun to fly Tony to New Hampshire rather than drive. Tom made me the navigator, which was a mistake. He said, "We will follow the railroad tracks as far as we can and when we get in New Hampshire we will look for Lake Winnipesaukee." I kept a sharp eye out for the lake and finally spotted it. After flying over it for a few minutes we realized it was not Lake Winnipesaukee but the Atlantic Ocean! We made a quick 180° turn, found our airport and dropped Tony off so he could be in school with his older brother Hank. Flying with Tom was always an adventure.

CHAPTER 5

*"A young man who does not have what it takes
to perform military service is not likely to have
what it takes to make a living."*

JOHN F. KENNEDY

Early in 1965 I joined the Vermont Army National Guard. My draft number was fairly high and I wanted to finish my education at the University of Vermont. I joined as a medic because I'd had two years of premed at the University which qualified me to dissect a frog, but not much else. One of the officers, a major, grabbed me as his driver because he wanted me to go to Officer Candidate School. As I drove him around to various meetings at our summer camp, he brought me into all the meetings so I could witness what was going on within the Vermont Army National Guard. At that point I was thinking maybe I would go to OCS, however, I really hadn't made up my mind for sure. Because of the Vietnam War there was a shortage of basic training spaces for National Guard soldiers. Fourteen of us were picked to go to a special basic training course at Fort Dix with the idea that when we returned after 19 weeks, we would go to OCS. After basic training we went off to our advanced training at the Fort Knox tanker school. Most of the training was a lot of fun and I really enjoyed driving and shooting the tanks. However, when I got home I changed my mind about going to OCS and opted to stay as an enlisted man. After a year or so as a tanker I became an artillery gunner and eventually transferred into the 40th Army Band as a trumpet player. I finished my 38 years in the National Guard after serving as First Sergeant for 24 years.

Dave driving the Fiat Jolly to Miami

During the summer of 1965 Dad drove me over to Plattsburgh Air Force Base where I caught a military hop to Westover Air Force Base in Massachusetts, another hop to Andrews Air Force Base in Delaware, and another hop to Homestead Air Force Base near Miami. I then hitched rides as far as Fort Lauderdale, FL where Tom drove down and picked me up. He had asked me to come down because he had a couple of jobs for me to do. Puddin' had a stable of cars among which was a Fiat Jolly which was made from 1955 to 1969. The car had no doors and wicker seats with a fringe top. She wanted the car driven to Miami so she could ship it to Hawaii where she was going to spend the summer. I must say it was a lot of fun driving the little car down the interstate from Palm Beach to Miami, where Tom picked me up to bring me back to Palm Beach. She also owned a Facel Vega, a small Italian sports car with a huge Chrysler engine in it. She wanted me to drive the car from Palm Beach to Beverly Hills, CA so her brother could sell it with the hope of getting more money there than they would get in Palm Beach. The car was sold originally as a standard shift but she had converted it to an automatic shift, so it didn't have a park position on the shifting column. Also, the parking brake had worn out. I received a lot of funny looks when I pulled up to a parking place, jumped out of my very expensive sports car to put a rock under the back tire so the car wouldn't roll away. The car went like crazy and I remember racing a tornado across Texas where I tried to lean out the window to take a picture as I was driving about 100 miles an hour. It was quite a trip with fun stops in New Orleans, Houston to watch a ballgame, El Paso, and Las Vegas before I got to Beverly Hills. I stopped in Houston to see a ballgame at the Astrodome because Puddin' was married to Craig Cullinan who was one of the developers of the ballpark.

In 1962, Dad had gone to Lake Chapleau in Canada to fish with some friends. Dad had caught many fish and had lots of fun so Tom and I decided to bring the three boys and Andre, the chef, to the lake to fish in the summer of 1966. We had a great time catching Brook Trout and Lake Trout. About that time Tom decided he would move on and try some other line of work. He retired from working for Puddin' gradually, helping her a few times after he retired. One sad time he flew to Hawaii after her youngest son Jeffrey had drowned while surfing.

CHAPTER 6

*"If you live in New York, even if
you're Catholic, you're Jewish."*

LENNIE BRUCE

MARX SERVICES INTERNATIONAL

Marx Services International was started by Tom in 1966. He rented an apartment at 350 East 51st Street in New York City and sent out fliers to try to drum up business delivering important papers or doing personal errands for the rich and famous. He wasn't very busy, but he worked hard for a couple of years trying to build the business. One of his neighbors was Samantha Jones who was in the movie *Wait Until Dark*, starring Audrey Hepburn and Alan Arkin. It made for some interesting conversations when they met in the hallway.

I was away at basic training at Fort Dix, New Jersey. What a treat that was! However, on the one weekend we had off, Jim White, the Bennington County Forester, and I took the bus to New York and stayed at Tom's apartment for the weekend. It was very relaxing to get away from the drill instructors, even for one night. When I finished basic training, I took a bus to New York and stayed for a couple of days with Tom. He said I should take the helicopter from the top of the Pan Am building (now the Met Life building) over to the airport to catch my flight home. That was quite a thrill. The helicopter hovered over a giant fan and quickly lifted up off the top of the building which was 60 stories in the air! That was quite a flight. I don't think I would want to do it again. A few years later in the early 1970s, the helicopter crashed while taking off from the top of the building killing four people in the helicopter and one person on the ground.

When I got home from basic training, I had graduated from the University of Vermont, bought my first car, a 1963 Volkswagen, and had gone to work for General Electric as a production control specialist. Tom was still trying to make Marx Services International profitable but it wasn't looking good. We were both ready for a new challenge.

Part II The Business Years

Malmar Tree Farms

CHAPTER 7

"Never worry about the size of your Christmas tree. In the eyes of children, they are all 30 feet tall."

LARRY WILDE

The business years lasted roughly from 1966 until 1992. During that time, Tom and I established and ran four businesses: Malmar Tree Farms, Malmar Vexar Cones, Power Petroleum Incorporated, and Malmar Property Management.

Our first business was Malmar Tree Farms. It was during the summer of 1966 that Tom and I went out to look for some land. Tom's brother-in-law, Bob Ray, owned the Plymouth dealership in Burlington with his father. He loaned us a 1948 Plymouth to use. We planned on staying at a small hunting lodge in Fayston, VT called TARhoff - meaning house of Tom, Angelo, and Remo. It was a cozy little hunting lodge owned by Tom, Angelo Pizzagalli, and his brother Remo. We drove around the middle of Vermont and looked at a number of pieces of land, all of which were either too small or overpriced. We arrived back at the camp, cooked our dinner, and relaxed. Tom said he wanted to go out and see some deer. We were staying close to an apple orchard that Dad and I had hunted many times. So we drove over to the apple orchard, walked through the apple trees and seated ourselves on a stone fence. We had been sitting there for about 20 minutes when I heard a slight noise. I slowly turned and saw a doe standing right behind Tom. I motioned for him to turn around slowly. As he did, the doe realized that Tom didn't belong there and they were both startled. I don't know who was more surprised, Tom or the doe. When I saw the expression on Tom's face I started laughing because the deer was a lot closer than Tom had expected or wanted it to be.

Ed Brown told us about a fellow who had some land for sale in Canaan, VT near the Quebec and New Hampshire border. Ed was a friend from the University of Vermont who owned about half the shoreline of Little Averill Lake in Norton, VT. Ed and I used to go to his camp on the lake to fish in the summer and to hunt in the winter. Off we went to look at the land. It was owned by Alfonse Sage and it was supposed to be 500 acres for $4000. We climbed the hills and roamed around walking a good portion of the land and it looked, to us, to be really nice. We thought we should have somebody look at it to see if we could make any money selling some Christmas trees or timber. Remo had hired a forester, Galen Hutchinson, to work on his tree farms, so we borrowed him and had him look at the land. He chained the boundaries, meaning he did a rough survey, and came back and told us it was only about 400 acres not 500. However, he said it was full of Christmas trees and we could probably sell trees for the rest of our lives. We went back and argued with Alfonse about the price per acre but he held firm so we bought it anyway. Alfonse was known to be a little shady about getting goods into and out of Canada, and also kind of stretched the truth about almost everything. He thought he had screwed us because he had cut most of the timber off the land. He didn't realize the value of the Christmas trees and we sure didn't tell him. It was a handshake deal and Alfonse was true to his word. He found out the value of the Christmas trees before the closing and offered us $5000 at the closing, but we said no.

Later that summer, Galen and I drove up to the land one weekend to work on the trees. We didn't have a place to stay on the farm so we stayed at the North Country Inn in Canaan. It was quite a wild place on Friday nights because they had a dance for all the farmers, so we didn't get much sleep that night. We spent that weekend mostly looking at the property and seeing what was there. It was quite impressive. We had trees of all sizes and most of it was softwood. We had acres and acres of Christmas trees in all stages of growth. We realized we could spend many days pruning and shearing trees to get them ready for the market. It was almost overwhelming. On the way home we decided to stop in and see Alfonse. Galen had purchased a used four wheel drive jeep from the US Border Patrol. When we stopped in to see Alfonse we thought he was going to faint because he thought the Border Patrol was coming after him. Being a smuggler, he always lived in fear of getting caught and he thought his time was up. After a short visit with Alfonse, Galen and I drove away and talked about the experience all the way home.

Tom and I joined the Vermont-New Hampshire Christmas Tree Association and we also registered our land as a tree farm. For the rest of the year, Galen and I stayed in his tent every weekend that we went to the farm to work on the trees. During the summer we spent our time thinning out many clumps of Christmas trees. They were just so thick that they had no room to grow. In the fall we went to the land to cut Christmas trees to sell. One night we were staying in Galen's tent and I heard a wild screeching sound. I jumped out of my sleeping bag, grabbed my shotgun, and ran out of the tent. I was sure that a mountain lion or some coyotes were coming to get us. Galen woke up and started laughing at me. He said, "Dave, it's just a screech owl. Go back to sleep!" That first year we cut trees that didn't look too bad and tied them up with baling twine to get them ready for market. Galen said a lot of our wild trees were "TV trees," meaning you could put your Christmas tree in front of your television and still watch the program!

After spending many nights in Galen's tent I really didn't want to spend any more weekends in it. Tom and I decided we would look for something a little better. Tom heard about a 38-foot house trailer for sale in Randolph, VT. He went down and talked the owner into selling the trailer to us for less than he owed on it. Good old Tom. We borrowed one of Pizzagalli's pickup trucks and went to Randolph to pick up the trailer. We hitched the trailer to the pickup and headed off for Canaan. We were all over the road with the darn thing because the trailer was too heavy for the pickup. We finally got to Canaan and started up the steep hill on our land. Once we got off level ground the pickup just could not pull the trailer. We left the truck and trailer and went to see the farmer across the street from our land. His name was Paul Harvey, no relation to the broadcaster, and asked him if he could help us get the trailer onto our land. Paul had a big diesel David Brown tractor which he brought to our truck. We hitched up the tractor to the pickup and started up the hill. Now at this point, I have to say, I expected the tractor to just go up the hill with no problem. However, I was wrong. The tractor couldn't move the truck and the trailer up the hill either. Paul had the solution. He went to get his hired hand with another diesel David Brown tractor. We hitched the other tractor in front of the first tractor but we still couldn't pull everything up the hill. At this point, we got a little smarter. We blocked up the trailer, unhitched the pickup, put the two tractors onto the trailer, and up the hill we went. We got to a nice level, open spot and parked the trailer. It would serve us well for the four years that we owned the farm. Every year we would go to the farm, work on the trees, cut them, sell them, and live in relative comfort. We always left the trailer unlocked and a few times people moved in and used it. Rumors from the area said that some of the hippies from the commune lived there once in a while and also a prisoner stayed there one summer. Apparently the police never suspected that he was living in our trailer and never caught him.

CHAPTER 8

Balsam inner bark is a natural pain
depressant similar to Ibuprofen.

Folk Medicine

At this point Tom and I figured we didn't have enough to do. Later I will talk about our other businesses, but will stay with the tree farms for now. In 1968 we purchased a 200-acre tree farm in North Wolcott, VT for $25 an acre. If you have ever been in North Wolcott you might not have even known you were in it! The North Wolcott Farm was unique. It was actually two joined parcels of land. The parcel on the main road in town was owned by the local preacher, Wendell Capron, and included his house. Wendell wanted to keep his house so we just purchased the land in back. The other portion of the property was located on a back road and also contained a house owned by Norman Rockwell, not the painter. He was happy to sell his house with the land. That was handy for us because it gave us access to the land from two different sides. The upper portion of the land contained a quaking bog where the vegetation forms an umbrella cover on the water over a period of many years. This umbrella mat was quite thick and you could actually walk on the top of it. As you were walking, it would "quake." Since these bogs were quite rare, Max McCormick, a University of Vermont forester, was quite interested in the bog. It contained many unusual plants such as insect eating plants like Pitcher Plants and Sundew, as well as wild Water Lilly. Once the bog was discovered, it was visited by many classes from various schools. One time I brought an iron rod that was 8 feet long, poked it into the bog and never touched bottom.

We really didn't know what to do with the house that came with the land. It was quite run down but still livable. A hippie group approached us and wanted to rent the house. That sounded good to us because it would give us a little income from the property, so we rented it to the group. The hippies didn't believe in mail, so I had to stop in every month to pick up the rent. However, in the summer, picking up the rent was not so bad. All the girls loved to work outside in the garden topless, so picking up the rent was actually rather pleasant.

During the first year that the hippies rented our house the local FBI agent contacted me and said that the daughter of a famous national news reporter was living in our house. She was suspected of being involved in the Weathermen terrorist group which also included Timothy Leary and Bill Ayers, a friend of Barack Obama. My job was to keep track of her and report to the FBI on her activities. It was a very interesting job and gave me more reasons to stop in to see the girls!

Of course, the real reason for the tree farm was the trees. There was a large field, about 30 acres, in back of Wendell's house that needed trees. We hired Galen, the forester, to advise us on what to do. He said we should plant Christmas trees, so we planted Balsam Fir, Concolar Fir, Frazier Fir, Scotch Pine and White Pine. The proper spacing of about 6' x 6' meant that we could plant about 1200 trees per acre. All the trees were planted by hand - Galen, his helper, and I. Planting the trees required the use of a planting bar. The bar was about 3½ feet long, with a handle on the top and a spur about 15 inches from the bottom where there was a sharp spade. In order to plant a tree we would step on the spur, push it in the ground, wiggle it back and forth to open up a spot, and drop the tree into the hole. We carried about 200 trees in a small canvas bag over our shoulder. After the tree was put in the hole, we would stamp the ground up around the tree and move onto the next one. We could each plant about 1200 trees per day. We planted the majority of trees as Balsam Fir because they have a wonderful aroma and they retain their needles longer. The state and federal governments had a refor-estation program that gave us the trees at a very cheap price. They were about five years old and were in very good condition.

Arlo Sterner was the Lamoille County forester where our North Wolcott farm was located. He was an old-time Vermonter, set in his ways, and couldn't stand flatlanders (people from Massachusetts, Connecticut, and Rhode Island). However, he was very good to people who would work with him. If you called him from out-of-state and asked him to do some tree work, it never seemed to get done. However, if you stopped into his office and asked him if he wanted to go out and work on the trees, off we would go. He and I spent many happy days working on government programs called TSI or Timber Stand Improvement and also working on the Christmas trees. We would go through the forest and mark the trees that he felt needed to be cut out so the good trees could grow into timber. I would go back on other days with a chainsaw and either cut down the smaller trees or girdle the big trees so they would eventually die.

One day Galen, Tom, and I went to the farm to do some work. Galen and I were cutting out gray birch so the Christmas trees would have room to grow and we told Tom to come along behind us and paint the stumps so they wouldn't grow back again. When Galen and I came back, Tom had painted all of the stumps with orange boundary paint. He was quite proud of his work! However, he was supposed to paint them with 2,4,5,T, a very potent toxin to kill the stumps. We had acres of very pretty orange stumps which would eventually grow back. I have to say Tom tried very hard; however, Galen did pick on him unmercifully for many years.

CHAPTER 9

*"The Northeast Kingdom region of Vermont has many
lakes, ponds, and farms and is the most rural
and unique part of Vermont."*

VERMONT TRAVEL GUIDE

The tree farms were never a big source of income, but they were fun and we made money on the land sales. We met many wonderful people through the different associations and learned much about nature. Our farm in Canaan was three hours away, so we couldn't just go for the day and expect to get much done. However Galen and I went up every fall and cut Christmas trees. Dustin Day had a truck and he would pick up our trees and sell them on the wholesale market. The Canaan farm was beautiful. We could stand on the top of the hill and see Quebec and New Hampshire. I spent quite a few days hunting and fishing on our farm or near it. We had many deer and bear on our land, as well as an assortment of small game. One day Ed Brown, who had told us about the land originally, called and said he had a guy interested in buying the land. Ed had his real estate license and that was the only time we used a realtor to buy or sell any of our properties. We were able to save a lot of money in real estate fees by finding our own buyers. The interested buyer was offering $100 per acre. Since we had paid $10 an acre four years earlier and being smart University of Vermont business graduates, we said we could be talked into selling the land. That was a nice profit for a couple of single guys and it gave us some investment money. Even our parents were impressed.

We had one last chore to do before selling the land. Being good caretakers of the property we wanted to go get the trailer off the hill. Back to Paul Harvey and his David Brown tractor.

Alfonse had said he wanted the trailer for his hired man to live in. As I said before, we had always left the trailer unlocked and at various times people stayed there. I think one of the people was the hired man who worked for Alfonse. He knew the trailer and liked it. The trailer was the old style with the rounded back. We told Alfonse he could have the trailer for $200. As Paul was hauling it down the hill, the back of the trailer was rubbing on the ground every time we went over a bump. If you can remember the old sardine cans with a twist off key you can picture what the back of the trailer was doing as we brought it down the hill. The metal was peeling up the back just like the sardine cans. When we got to the bottom of the hill we borrowed a hammer and some nails from Paul, pulled the metal back down and nailed it back to the trailer. We had borrowed another one of Pizzagalli's trucks, hitched up the trailer to the truck, and said our goodbyes to Paul with a vow that he would never tell Alfonse about the trailer. Alfonse used that trailer for his hired man until he died many years later.

North Wolcott was quite a bit more accessible. We had bought the land and the house in 1968. We had planted about 20,000 trees in the field behind town and had quite a bit of timber and many marketable Christmas trees in the back part of the land. Every year I would cut my own Christmas tree as well as a few for friends, which included the Reverend Richard Crocker at the Underhill Congregational Church. I would always try to come within a few inches of the church ceiling with the Christmas tree. We also found an old sugar house full of metal sap buckets and sold as many as we could carry out. We gave some of them to Tom's sister, Joyce, who painted them and sold them in various markets. I still have one of them in my office, which reminds me of our fun days as Christmas tree farmers. Every year we sold off enough trees and some timber to pay the taxes, but like Canaan, because of our other businesses we never had enough time to do a proper job maintaining the property. One side benefit was that Dad and I spent many days on the tree farm hunting deer and we were quite successful.

We had lost the chance to rent the house to the hippies, which was very disappointing to me, but we found a guy who wanted to buy it. Lynn Gribbin paid us $5000 for the house and

10 acres and usually sent us a check every month for the next ten years. Sometimes if Lynn was a little behind in the rent, I would stop in and collect it and do some fishing in a trout stream near the house. Lynn eventually sold five acres to a guy from New York who put up a small house where we used to hunt.

CHAPTER 10

"The perfect Christmas tree?
All Christmas trees are perfect. "

CHARLES N. BARNARD

B eing industrious does not always bring the best results. Over the years, Tom and I found that sometimes being smart helps also. I think it is safe to say that not many of my readers have ever tied Christmas trees by hand to get them ready for shipping. It is not a lot of fun. The process involves a role of bailing twine like farmers use for tying up their bales of hay, a pair of sharp shears, and a dumb person. On our Canaan tree farm, I was the dumb person. The first year we had the farm, Galen and I went to the farm to cut and tie trees for market. Galen was the smart guy. He would go into a large clump of balsam trees, pick out the good ones that he thought would sell, and cut them down. The dumb guy, me, would drag the trees out to the road. When I had eight or ten trees lined up on the road, I would begin to tie them up. I will try to walk you through this process: cut three or four long pieces of the bailing twine, depending on the size of the Christmas tree; lay the pieces of twine on the road about 2 feet apart; lift the tree and lay it on the pieces of twine. Now the fun begins. Jump onto the tree at the big end and squeeze the branches together with your legs, at the same time reach down for the two ends of the twine, bring them up around the tree and tie the branches as tightly as possible. Repeat the process from the big end of the tree up to the small end. I have to say that those guys who ride the bucking bulls had nothing on me! Galen and I would do this all day Saturday and half the day on Sunday before we would head for home. By Sunday Noon I could hardly stand, to say nothing of trying to walk.

This is where the smart guy thing comes in. Tom and I had read about a process where Christmas trees could be dragged through a big funnel and wrapped in a plastic net for shipping. We knew a metal fabricator in Burlington, Danny Provost, and asked him to draw up some plans to make some big funnels to pull the Christmas trees through. We told him that DuPont was making a plastic wrap called Vexar which would fit over the end of the cones. All we would have to do is pull the trees through the cones butt first, stretching the netting over the butt of the tree, and when the tree was completely through the cone, cut the netting at the end of the tree and presto, the tree was wrapped and ready for shipping! Danny came up with a plan for five different cone sizes. He thought that an eight inch cone would be about the smallest we would use and a sixteen inch cone would probably take care of almost any big Christmas tree. We told him to go ahead and build the five different sizes. We managed to find an old trailer, took the box off it, covered the bed with plywood, and mounted a 10 inch, a 12 inch, and a 14 inch cone on it. We were in business.

I mentioned a few pages ago that we had joined the Vermont- New Hampshire Christmas tree Association and had registered our two farms as tree farms. This gave us access to many people who were growing and selling Christmas trees. We had a Chevrolet Corvair van for our gasoline business, so we put a trailer hitch on it and dragged our trailer around the state showing everybody our Vexar cones. We had good success going to the meetings and selling cones to the growers.

CHAPTER 11

"Lumberjacks are crazy people.
They swing from trees like a monkey and
mangle arms and legs with axes and chain saws. "

Unknown

The Lumberjack Roundup was held in Vermont at Lake Dunmore every summer. It was a fun event which I always went to and sometimes Tom would go with me. Lumberjacks from around the world would come to compete at the Roundup. People such as Dave Geer and Sven Johnson would always show up and compete in events such as log sawing, pole climbing, log chopping, and ax throwing. We always had a ball watching the competition. Many times they would have events for the kids such as trying to catch a greased pig. Nobody ever caught the pig! Many times I would bring our trailer with the cones and try to sell a few of them, but some years I would just pass out our business cards. One year somebody entered Tom in the log sawing contest. Arlo Sterner, our friend and Lamoille County forester, was in charge of the competition and kept yelling, "Tom Marx, Tom Marx, report to the competition area." It was a joke and we never did find out who entered Tom in the competition, but I still think it was Jim White, my friend, the Bennington County forester. Arlo was pretty mad at us but he got over it when he found out we hadn't done it. He knew it wasn't Tom's fault and it wasn't Tom's forte either. However, I entered an amateur crosscut sawing contest for a few years with a friend and won the competition two years in a row in Underhill at the Harvest Market.

Dave and Rich Staab after winning log sawing contest

I also brought our trailer to various other meetings of Christmas tree growers in Vermont and New Hampshire and we sold quite a few cones at those meetings. We had some very big growers near our Canaan farm such as Lorraine Marchessault, and near our Wolcott farm like John Young and Joe Trombly. They bought the cones and loved them which helped to sell the cones to some of the other big growers in the different associations; eventually most of the growers were using our cones.

From the mid-1960s through the 1970s, all three of our businesses were running at the same time: the two tree farms, the Vexar cones and Power Petroleum. This made for some interesting conflicts. My job in the oil business was sales, so I was on the road. This allowed me to stop in at our farm in Wolcott to do some tree work or boundary marking and sometimes even a little fishing while still getting my calls done for the oil business. One day Tom was in Montreal, another day off, so he was away from the office. Since there were only two of us in the business, that meant that I was in the office manning the phones and paying the bills. I had a couple of deliveries to make and when I got back to the

38

office I had a call from Jim White, the Bennington County forester, asking me to come to a meeting of Christmas tree growers that afternoon. He wanted me to bring the trailer with the cones on it because some of the growers were interested in buying a cone or two. Vermont is not considered a big state, however, it is 110 miles from our office to Jim's office, and so I hooked up the trailer and drove down to Jim's office. I ended up selling one cone, visited for a few minutes with Jim, and drove home. Tom came back from Montreal, stopped by the office and discovered that we had had a delivery of filters and the trucker had just left all the boxes outside of our warehouse in the driveway. Tom opened the office, put the boxes in the warehouse, immediately called me and chewed me out. He was very upset that I had left the warehouse with nobody there. That is the only time in our many years of business that we had a serious argument. Tom was right to be mad but my job was sales and I felt we could make a sale. As it turned out, it was not a good business decision.

The Vexar cone business was interesting and we were able to make a small profit which paid for our own cones, our trailer, and with the sale of timber and Christmas trees, the taxes and the expenses on our tree farms. Along the way we met many different people and learned a unique business.

CHAPTER 12

"Phillips Petroleum was founded in 1917 by Frank and L. E. Phillips. The 66 was added in 1927 when a vehicle was testing their new high octane gasoline and reached a speed of 66 miles per hour on route 66."

PHILLIPS PETROLEUM ARCHIVES

In 1965 most people had not heard of Donald Trump with his big ego and funny hair. However, there was a major oil company which also had a big ego at that time. Texaco Oil Company had built gasoline stations in all of the 50 states and loved to brag about it. "You can trust your car to the man who wears the star" was seen and heard throughout the country. Phillips 66 also had a big ego and was quite upset by being outdone by Texaco. Phillips did not have any stations in northern New England where Texaco was very well represented. A corporate decision was made to expand to Maine, New Hampshire, and Vermont. Phillips approached Pizzagalli Construction and asked them to build gasoline stations on land which they had purchased or leased. When Pizzagalli had finished building three stations, Phillips approached them and asked if they would be interested in starting a "scratch jobber-ship." Angelo Pizzagalli told Phillips that he might be interested but he wanted to think it over. Angelo asked his good friend Tom what he thought of the idea. Tom thought it over and told Angelo it sounded interesting and challenging. And that is how Power Petroleum was born. The three Pizzagalli brothers, three other local businessmen and Tom said they would begin operations in October of 1967. At that time Phillips had been running the stations directly with Terry Sousa as the district salesman. Tom rented a small office and a small warehouse space from Bernie Rocheleau in South Burlington just down the street from the Pizzagalli Construction warehouse. Tom, with the help of Terry, ordered an initial supply of tires, batteries, accessories, oil, and antifreeze from Phillips and went to work. Initially Tom's job was to supply the three gasoline stations which Phillips had built with all of the Phillip's products, including gasoline. He hired Merrill Transport to haul all the gasoline from Rensselaer, New York. Phillips had an exchange agreement with Hess Oil Company and for the five years that we were in business we never sold a single gallon of Phillips 66 gasoline. We didn't know it at the time, but this arrangement was common even though Phillips advertised their products in our area.

Tom could not keep up with the paperwork and still go out to sell product, to say nothing about trying to get new accounts. At the time I was wandering around at General Electric wondering who was doing my job because I never found out what I was supposed to be doing! I was told I was in charge of ordering parts for the Vulcan mini gun which GE was manufacturing. The fellow who was supposed to train me for my job had pneumonia when I went to work there and never came back to work. No one ever told me, in the three months that I was there, what parts I was supposed to be ordering; however, somebody must have been doing it because they never ran out! I had been looking at two different jobs because I wanted to get out of GE. Frank Dion had offered me a job as a stockbroker at his firm. Bob Candy had also offered me a job as his assistant in the information and education department of the Vermont Fish and Wildlife Department. Unfortunately Bob said I had to move to Montpelier in order to do the job so I turned it down. I then turned my attention to Frank and his job. Both jobs would have been interesting and fun; however, about that time Tom came along and asked me to be a salesman for Power Petroleum. To the rescue again! Much to the dismay of my father, I took the job with Tom. At that point I was young and single and thought that the job would be fun and challenging.

So there we sat, Tom and I, in a rented office with a rented warehouse full of tires, batteries, oil, various other products, the

1964 Corvair van that Tom had purchased from Puddin, and my Volkswagen bug. What to do! Our accounts consisted of three gasoline stations and Pizzagalli Construction of which we were a subsidiary. They bought their gasoline, diesel fuel, and motor oil from us. Well, I have to say, we certainly didn't have enough customers to keep two guys busy nor enough cash flow to pay expenses and us a salary.

Tom had been doing all the paperwork for Phillips, keeping the bills paid, and keeping the banks happy. I started out at the office so I could learn the paperwork in case there was too much for Tom or in case he was gone, which later on, was often the case! However, we figured that I should collect the money and the credit card slips from the stations and at the same time see what I could sell to them for gasoline, oil, and accessories. When I was finished with the three stations, I would go to Pizzagalli to see if they needed any product. Then I would go back to the office with my orders, write them up, drive the van around to the back of the building to our warehouse, and put all the orders together. If one of the stations was almost out of some supplies, such as light bulbs or fan belts or oil or tires, I would load the order into the van and deliver it right away. If not, I would get all the orders together and deliver them the next day. I was always hoping that nobody needed a 55 gallon drum of oil or anti-freeze. We made a lot of money on the drums but at 450 pounds for the oil and 550 pounds for the antifreeze they were not fun to deliver. We used two planks as a ramp which we would rest on the ground and the inside of the van. The next step was the fun part. We would roll the drums up the planks and into the van. If Tom wasn't around, which sometimes happened, I would roll them into the van alone. That was always fun to see. Sometimes we were able to borrow a forklift from our landlord to load the drums, which was a huge help. Our van could hold up to three drums plus the other items I had sold. Delivering the drums was easy. We had an old truck tire that we carried around in the van and when we delivered the drums we would just roll them out of the van and bounced them off the truck tire onto the ground. Piece of cake!

When all of that was done, I had three days left to fill. Tom was busy processing the credit cards, paying Phillips for our product, and paying Merrill's for the trucking. At that point, since I knew a little about the paperwork at the office we sent Tom off to the Phillips dealer school to learn about the products and how to run a gasoline station. While he was gone, I answered the phone and took care of the paperwork in the office. When Tom came back he took over the office again and I went out to try to round up some new business. One funny thing that we did, at least it was funny to us, was sending the credit card slips to Phillips. They supplied envelopes to us which held about 50 of the credit card slips. We would fill up the envelopes, put two eight cent stamps on the envelopes and drop them in the mail. In the five years that we were in business, we sent thousands of dollars' worth of credit card invoices to Phillips and it wasn't until the last three months of our business that they sent us a nasty letter and told us to put on the correct amount of postage. Over the 4¾ years we saved hundreds of dollars in postage.

One way to drum up new business was to buy or use products from the business we wanted to sell our products to. We went to Avis rent a car and rented two cars from them to use in our business. We leased a station wagon for my use which allowed me to carry product around while making calls. This often saved me from having to run back to the warehouse. We also rented a sedan for Tom. We told Avis that they should buy our oil because we were using their cars and they agreed. Avis was our first new customer. Yea for us! We also went to our landlord because he had the Winnebago franchise for our area and used a lot of oil. He also agreed to use our product. We were just growing by leaps and bounds.

CHAPTER 13

"Phillips developed the pointy canopy in the 1950's. It was also called "Bat wing" and the "Butterfly."

PHILLIPS PETROLEUM ARCHIVES

One innovation by Phillips that was not done by any of the other oil companies was to put a vacuum cleaner next to the gas pumps. All of our dealers were instructed to open the driver's door and vacuum out the inside of the car. The reason for that was so they could look at the oil sticker on the driver's door and see if it was time for an oil change. An additional reason, and also a bonus, was if there was a pretty girl driving the car the dealer could get a good look at her. This of course very seldom happened. They were also instructed to wash the windows and check the oil. They would take the dipstick from the car and show it to the customer. If the oil was down or if it was time for an oil change the dealer would suggest adding oil or doing an oil change right there. While the hood was up the dealer also checked the antifreeze and fan belts. This led to a lot of sales and helped both the dealer and his friendly distributor.

Another thing that Phillips insisted on was being open every day of the year including Christmas and New Year's. What they didn't tell us was how many hours they had to be open. Since Tom and I were both single and sometimes it was difficult to get one of our married dealers to work on a major holiday, Tom and I both spent many holiday mornings pumping gas at one of our stations in order to satisfy the Phillips requirement. However, we would usually only stay open for a few hours then close up and go home.

Phillips was so excited to get us signed up to sell their product that they gave us the whole state of Vermont as our territory.

Although Vermont is only 120 miles long and 90 miles wide at the widest point, we soon discovered that it was much easier and more cost-effective to service the area closest to our warehouse. That led to some problems with Phillips later on.

Phillips had named the three stations which they had built. Hilltop 66 was in Winooski right next to the interstate and was a prime location. Cloverleaf 66 was in South Burlington and was also next to the interstate and also a prime location. Country Club 66 was in Burlington on Shelburne Road and was right next door to Dunkin' Donuts. All three stations were constructed with the famous Phillips pointed canopy. Phillips was one of the first companies to put canopies on their stations to keep their customers from getting wet when it was raining or snowing, which seemed to be most of the time in Vermont.

One of Tom's favorite sayings whenever we helped somebody out and they thanked us was to say, "It's all part of our friendly service." One day when I was collecting the money at Country Club 66, four older ladies drove in with a broken spring. They were very upset because they had driven over from New York to spend the day at the Shelburne Museum. I offered to bring them to the museum and pick them up later in the afternoon when they were done. They just couldn't believe that I would be willing to do that. The Shelburne Museum was about 10 miles from our station and really not a long drive to drop the four ladies off. We made arrangements to pick them up about 2:00 p.m. I went about my business for the day and went down at two o'clock to pick them up. They were very excited at having spent the day at the museum and having me pick them up to bring them back to their car that had been fixed. I told them, "It's all part of our friendly service." They asked me who they should write to in order to thank the company for my service. I told them to write to Mr. Thomas Marx at the Power Petroleum office. They wrote a beautiful letter which I saved.

215-39 46th Avenue
Bayside, New York 11361

July 14, 1968

Power Petroleum Inc.
Burlington, Vermont

Dear Sir:

    This letter is being written unequivocally in praise
of one of your customer representatives, David L. Mallory.

    Last Sunday evening, July 7th, while driving near Shel-
burne, our car developed some trouble. We drove into your
Country Club 66 station for assistance to learn that we had
a broken spring. Since it couldn't be repaired that evening,
we made an appointment to return early the next morning.

    Needless to say, we felt rather discouraged at the delay
in our vacation trip and the rather gloomy prospect of spending several hours waiting at the gas station during the repair job.

    However, when we returned (there were four adults in the
group), Mr. Mallory was in the office, and, after discovering
our dilemma, immediately offered his services to us and suggested that he drive us to Shelburne Museum to wait out our
stay. We had already seen some of the exhibits the day before but were more than anxious for a return visit, so the
suggestion was most welcome.

    Not only did he drive us there at 9 A.M. but returned
for us promtly at the appointed hour 2 P.M.---and it's a con-
siderable distance of several miles---a sizable sum on any
New York taxi meter!

    Mr. Mallory's manner was so outstandingly cheerful, friend-
ly and courteous, as to be completely disarming. He refused
to accept any remuneration for the favor, laughing it off as
"part of the friendly service of Phillips 66". To paraphrase
a quote--"You're in good hands" with men like Mr. Mallory on
your staff.

Sincerely yours,

(Miss) Hermine S. Pert

439
6.443

Letter from the four women from New York

Much of my time every week was spent knocking on doors trying to get new customers. After two or three times I finally signed a Shell customer in Waitsfield who was very unhappy with Shell Oil Company. Bob Moulton was a fussy, cantankerous guy from New York, but was extremely loyal if we kept him happy. We did! He had a great location at the base of two major Vermont ski areas. Glen Ellen and Mad River Glen were always very busy in the winter time and also were quite busy during the summer tourist season. Bob became our first new Phillips dealer and sold many truckloads of gasoline for us as well as many cases of oil and antifreeze. It was always fun to stop in every other week to collect the credit cards and money. Bob never held back his feelings so we always knew in a hurry if we had made any mistakes. In the years that we were in business he was the only dealer who would climb up on top of the tanker, open up the compartments, and check to make sure all of the gasoline had been delivered.

CHAPTER 14

Jericho Center is situated close to Interstate 89 and is an easy commute to IBM or Burlington.

VERMONT TRAVEL GUIDE

WELL BEFORE DAWN ON CHRISTMAS EVE, JUST LIKE ANY ORDINARY day, Lil Desso will rise from bed, get dressed, and go downstairs followed by two small dogs and a cat named Belvedere (all ex-strays official critters now on the premises) to open up the store. She'll meet the milk drop and make the coffee, put out the doughnuts and take in the newspapers. If it's snowing, she'll spread some rock salt on the steps before opening the door at five sharp. Someone is bound to be

Lil and Gerry Desso from Yankee Magazine

Jericho Center had one of the original old Vermont country stores that was built in the late 1700's just after the town was chartered. From that time until the mid-1960's only six owners had run the store. Gerry and Lil Desso took over the store in 1965 as the seventh owners. This was a real country store, selling a wide selection of items including saws and nails, fresh meat, canned goods, fresh donuts and coffee, greeting cards, tools, electrical supplies, plumbing supplies, and it even had a post office. If you needed something, they probably had it or could get it. I approached the Desso's about buying gasoline from us. Gerry informed me they only had a 500 gallon gas tank and it was under the cement of the front steps. This presented a problem to us because we only used tractor trailers to deliver our gasoline and we liked to deliver at least a half load to each customer which was close to 4000 gallons. Gerry was buying from Esso, but was unhappy with the delivery process because he often ran out of gas, so he was very interested in getting bigger tanks. They had a rather small area in front of the store in which to install gas tanks.

Myers Petroleum was owned by Walt Myers and we called upon him to solve our problem. Walt said that we couldn't dig up the 500 gallon tank without breaking up the cement leading into the store but he thought we could fill it up with sand and leave it there. He felt that he could put in a 4000 gallon tank and a 2000 gallon tank in front of the store. The Desso's agreed to sign up with us. One problem we had was to keep them supplied with gasoline in their 500 gallon tank until we were able to install their large tanks. We hired a local trucker with a small truck to keep them supplied with Mobil gasoline until we could get the tanks installed. I have to admit that they did run out of gasoline a few times and I got a couple of irate phone calls from Gerry wondering where his gas was. In the 1960s it cost us about $4000 to install the two tanks and put in two new pumps. That was a lot of money for our little company considering we made three cents a gallon on our gasoline. In today's market, we would have to put in two double walled tanks, two pumps, one being a blender because there are three products now, and the price would be between $45,000 and $50,000. Things sure have gotten expensive and it makes me glad, with the prices and the government regulations, that we are no longer in business. When we started putting in the tanks we had to dig up the front yard and tried to keep a little passage open so that people could still get into the store. We did have a few dicey moments and I did get a few more phone calls from Gerry, but over the years we developed a very good friendship. In 1972 I got married and moved into a house just down the road from the store. In 1989 they were featured in YANKEE magazine in an article entitled "Christmas in Jericho, Vermont". When I am in Vermont I still try to get together with Gerry and Lil. They are great people.

CHAPTER 15

"Whatever Happened to Baby Jane" led to the birth of the "psycho biddy" in horror/thriller films featuring older psychotic women like Betty Davis.

Things were going along well for our little business but we still were not making enough money to pay our expenses. Our salaries were $6000 each, which wasn't a lot in those days. We really needed to get more customers and cut our expenses. Tom had purchased the Chevy Van from Puddin which had been named "Baby Jane" after the 1962 movie entitled, *Whatever Happened to Baby Jane?* We decided to sell the van, turn in our two lease cars, and buy a new Chevy van. We also bought a used Plymouth station wagon for me to use to call on accounts and deliver small orders. The next expense which we thought we could eliminate was the cost of delivering our drums and cases of oil from the railroad freight cars to our warehouse. We had been using Welch Trucking to go down to the railroad yards to pick up the 40,000 pounds of oil and deliver it to us. Since we were a subsidiary of Pizzagalli Construction we were able to borrow a trailer from them and we rented the tractor from Merrill Transport.

We had no idea what we were getting into! I had driven a tractor once before but it didn't have a trailer behind it. I figured it wouldn't be a problem, just hitching up a trailer and dragging it along behind me. I drove the tractor trailer down the steep hill of Main Street to the rail yards then I was faced with a problem. I had to back the trailer up to the rail car! Well, this was something new. After several tries, I finally got the trailer backed up to the rail car and figured we were good to go. I was wrong. That is when the work began. I can honestly say that 40,000 pounds of oil is a lot of oil. Tom came down and we loaded all the cases and drums onto our trailer. It took us a number of hours and our arms were kind of limp when we finished. Now it was time to drive the tractor trailer back to our warehouse. Remember the steep Main Street hill I went down? I now was faced with the task of driving 40,000 pounds back up the hill. I prayed that I wouldn't have to stop at one of the traffic lights partway up the hill. God probably heard my prayers but thought it would be more fun to watch me trying to deal with a stop light halfway up. I sat there in a panic until the light turned green, raced the engine, popped the clutch, and hopped like a rabbit up the rest of the hill. Thankfully I didn't hear any horns tooting so I figured nothing had rolled out the back! When I made it to our warehouse, Tom and I unloaded the oil. Those were long tiring days. After doing that three or four times we went back to the "smart guy" thing again. We called the employment office and hired a couple of muscle guys to do the loading and unloading. We always helped them, but I have to admit I didn't mind letting them do most of the work.

During that fall of 1968, the other six owners gave Tom and me a chance to buy them out. Six of them had invested $2000 each and Tom had invested $3000. They would sell the company to us for $4000 each. We agreed to do that and I became a partner with Tom with the two of us being the only owners. Mom and dad came to my rescue and loaned me the money to pay the other owners. It was another one of the many times they loaned me money to buy land, a car, or a business. I always paid them back with interest.

That year we sold enough Purolator filters to qualify for a trip to Jamaica. Wow! We stayed at the Playboy club along with a couple of our dealers who had also qualified by buying their filters from us. Since the Playboy club was a long distance from any town, the Playboy Bunnies were allowed to mingle with the guests. One night our Bunny waitress was a very pretty girl whose mother was Jamaican and whose father was Chinese. I asked her when she got off work and she said 2:00 a.m. I asked her if we could meet and she agreed. All the guys were jealous.

After dinner, I went to my room to take a nap before meeting the Bunny. Can you believe I slept right through until morning? None of my "friends" came to my room to wake me up. Nice bunch of friends I had! Every meal after that, I checked the dining room to make sure she wasn't working. I really didn't want to face her again.

CHAPTER 16

"Lincoln Gap - awesome road to view fall foliage."

CRUISE CRITIC REVIEW

Our third year of business, 1969, came in like a lion. Our business was doing well; however, behind our back, Phillips was looking for other jobbers in Vermont. They built a new station in St. Albans, but instead of having us run it, they signed on McMahon Oil to run the station. Needless to say, we were not very happy with Phillips. Nonetheless, in their defense, we had not explored that part of the state which was near the Canadian border, so we let it go.

Meanwhile I signed up a new account with The Little Store of Hanksville. Every time I signed a new account Tom went to the Chittenden Bank to borrow the $4000 to put in the tanks and pumps. Each new account had its own loan and the Chittenden got to know us quite well. The Little Store of Hanksville was a fun account in a beautiful area of Vermont. It was near Camels Hump, one of the five mountains in Vermont over 4000 feet, and next to the Huntington River which was always great trout fishing. Sometimes after I delivered oil or antifreeze and picked up the credit cards and money, I would stop to do a little trout fishing. I would then drive over Lincoln Gap, another beautiful area especially in the fall, to Waitsfield to see Bob Moulton.

I continued to wander around our territory trying to pick up a few more customers and continue servicing the customers we had. Tom was doing his part by keeping the bills paid, barely, but we still needed to generate more money. That was my job! In my travels I noticed a new building going up in Essex Center. It looked like it was going to be a little mom-and-pop store so I stopped in to see the owners. Gene and Marceline were calling their store "The Market", and were hoping to draw their customers from all the developments in that area. They also hoped to draw the Sunday business from St. Pius X Catholic Church across the street. They thought since they were a new business and we were a new local business it would be fun to grow together. Back to the Chittenden went Tom and we again hired Myers Petroleum to install our tanks and pumps. When we dug the hole for the tanks the water table was quite high and there was quite a bit of water in the hole. When we dropped the tanks into the hole they actually floated! Walt Myers had the solution. We got Merrill Transport to stand by with a load of gas, put the tanks in the ground, filled them up with gas, covered them with dirt, poured the concrete, paved the yard, and told Gene to never run out of gas.

I continued to explore our territory within 40 to 50 miles around Burlington. This was about as far as we felt we could service reasonably well. Williston Vermont was a nice little town about 15 miles from Burlington with a beautiful golf course. The town was growing by leaps and bounds because IBM had built a plant in nearby Essex Junction. There was a small store at the four corners of the town called Larrow's Market, across the street from the church, down the street from the National Guard Armory, and right near the Williston Country Club. Tom was kept busy going to the bank to get money for all our new accounts. We were establishing a very good reputation with the Chittenden Bank but more importantly with the loan officers, which would come in very handy in a few years. Walt Myers was also becoming very familiar with us as we had him put in more tanks and pumps. Wayne sold a lot of product for us and became a good and loyal customer as did most of the people we signed up to do business with us.

As I said before, 1969 came in like a lion. Would you believe we signed up another new account? Lucky Spot was a truck stop using Mobil gasoline and was located right at the interstate exit in Richmond. Leo owned a restaurant which all the truckers loved as well as a variety store which was also busy. The good thing about this account was that it already had tanks and pumps so we didn't have to install any new equipment. Even so, in order to get him to switch he wanted his yard paved, which we agreed to do. It turned out to be about the same amount of money to install new tanks and pumps; again, Tom made another trip to the bank. Lucky Spot turned out to be one of our biggest customers during the three years we had the store as an account.

I was beginning to build a nice route which I did on Tuesdays. I would start at Cloverleaf 66, go to Larrow's Market, stop at Lucky Spot, drive to the Little Store of Hanksville, and go over Lincoln Gap to see Bob in Waitsfield. Things were coming along nicely and we felt that we might be even making a few dollars. What a surprise!

It was about this time that Tom and I started a tradition we still observe; we take each other out to dinner for our birthdays. During the first few years when we were not earning a lot of money, and since we both lived near Burlington, we went to Bove's Italian restaurant. " Babe" Bove was the bartender and he would greet all the regular customers with, "Everybody's been asking for you!" We went there often enough so that we got to know "Babe" well enough that he would sneak us through the kitchen from the back door and we didn't have to wait in the long line outside. He also allowed us to join the Burlington Downtown Athletic Club, a very exclusive club which included governors, senators, mayors, some sports figures, as well as many prominent Burlington doctors and lawyers. Bove's restaurant was the headquarters for the club. As the years went by, we branched out to many restaurants throughout the world, some of which will be mentioned later.

A result of living in Burlington for so many years was that I knew a great many people. I had gone to high school and college, was a member of the Vermont Army National Guard, played in a number of bands, and worked, until I retired, in the Burlington area. Dad had been a police commissioner, an alderman, and also worked all his life in the Burlington area so he also met many people and introduced me to the majority of them. Because of that, it seemed that everywhere Tom and I went I would meet somebody I knew. We went to Montreal to celebrate Tom's birthday at Altitude 737, a beautiful restaurant at the top of Place Ville Marie. Tom said, "Well, we finally are at a place where nobody knows you." Just then a man stopped by our table and said, "Aren't you Dave Mallory?" Tom and I both broke up laughing. It was one of my neighbors from Burlington. The same thing just happened recently in Boynton Beach, FL when a friend of mine popped out of one of the charter boats near our restaurant and hollered to Tom and me. Tom just couldn't get over it.

CHAPTER 17

"Four of the five towns in Grand Isle County are situated
on islands in Lake Champlain."

W e found out in early 1970 that we had actually earned a
profit for 1969. What a surprise that was! We immediately
raised our salaries to $6500 each. We were so extravagant!
All the same, we found out that Phillips Petroleum was running
around behind our backs again and signed Bradford Oil to a
contract to sell Phillips gasoline. Bradford Oil was given the whole
Eastern part of Vermont. Immediately, the Bradford owner,
George Pratt, built a Go Go station between Barre and Montpelier.
Even though we hadn't been able to develop that area yet, we
considered it part of our territory, not far from our Waitsfield location.
Tom and I were very upset with Phillips and sent a very strong letter
to the company president. We told him in no uncertain terms what
we thought of their tactics and how disappointed we were with
his company. We received a quick visit from Bill Efferts, the Phillips
territory manager, and Harold Jones, the assistant territory manager.
They were livid! Their point was that we had not developed that
territory, which was the same argument they used when they gave
away the northern part of the state to McMahon Petroleum. They
also said that it would actually help our business by having more
brand exposure in the rest of the state. Our argument was that
the station that Bradford Oil built was not a Phillips location at all,
but was an unbranded location which wouldn't help us a bit and
they probably wouldn't even buy the gasoline from Phillips. We also
said that we'd only been in business for a little over a year and a
half and that we had done a good job developing our territory
around the Burlington area. We felt that they were not giving us

a chance to develop more stations. After arguing for a time with neither side agreeing with the other we finally agreed to disagree and made them take us out to dinner. Our relationship with Phillips was somewhat strained for a while, but eventually we all got over it. We learned a valuable lesson from that experience. Big corporations are out to make a profit and they don't mind stepping on toes to make that profit. Being rather young and inexperienced businessmen, it was a valuable lesson we learned that day.

I was still riding around in our Plymouth station wagon looking for new accounts with pretty good success, but we still were not getting rich. One day as I was driving to our tree farm in North Wolcott to collect the rent and see the girls, I noticed a repair garage being built on Route 15 in Morrisville, Vermont. I stopped in to see Ray and talked with him about doing business with a local distributor rather than the big oil companies he had been talking to. I told him that I would be coming by every other week to bring him any product he might need and to collect the credit cards and the money. He liked that idea because the other companies wanted him to mail everything in to them and it was up to him to buy his oil, antifreeze, and accessories where he could find them. Tom went off to the bank again, got the loan, and we put in tanks and pumps for Ray. He never sold a lot of gas but it was a convenient location for me. When I finished with him I could run up to the tree farm and do some work or collect the rent or even go fishing, which was excellent in the Lamoille River as well as some of the smaller brooks around the farm.

During the summer of that year we heard about a Mobil gas station that was for sale in South Hero. We approached the dealer, Ernie Ross, and asked him about the station. Ernie told us that the station was owned by a man in Massachusetts. We asked Ernie if he would be willing to run the station for us if we bought it and he agreed; he would rather do business with people who lived in the area. We called the owner John in Massachusetts and made arrangements to meet him at the station. We had our meeting and he told us that the asking price for the station was $40,000. We agreed on the price, purchased the station, (another trip to the bank), and changed the brand from Mobil to Phillips. We called the station Island Service Center and set Ernie up in business. Ernie was a very likable guy from Tennessee who was a hard worker full of ambition, but was a chain smoker with a drinking problem. Nonetheless, everybody in the area liked him so he had a very good following. The station was in an excellent location on the corner of Route 2 and the road that went to the ferry between Vermont and New York State. The gasoline tax in New York was always higher than it was in Vermont so people coming from New York, or going back, would stop and buy gas from Ernie because it was cheaper. During the summer we could hardly keep gas in the tanks, but during the winter, when the ferry wasn't running, the gasoline sales dropped off considerably. Because Ernie was well-liked he was still able to keep busy doing automotive repairs which also helped us because he bought oil, antifreeze, fan belts, light bulbs, etc. from us. Another thing that helped Ernie and all of our dealers was that Vermont had an inspection law which said that every registered car had to be inspected twice a year. That law kept a lot of garage owners in business during the lean times.

I was on a roll. Don Turner built a garage in Milton next door to his wooden pallet business. He called and asked us to supply him with gasoline. Our name and reputation was getting around. Another trip to the bank and we set Don and Nancy up with their gasoline. I would stop in every other week to collect the money and credit cards. They were located on a back road and I often saw deer near their location, so during deer season I would always have a rifle in the car. I saw a nice buck the week before deer season one year but never saw him during the season.

In October of 1970 we discovered that we had sold our one millionth gallon of gasoline for the year. We were jumping for joy and decided we would have a celebration. In comparison, Champlain Oil, which is a Citgo and Shell distributor and the company that I retired from many years later, sells 1,000,000 gallons of product in 2 ½ days! However, we didn't know that when we were in business and we were very happy for our little company. Montreal is a large Canadian city about 100 miles from Burlington. The Montreal Canadians were a hockey team in the National Hockey League which many of us followed. Tom and I thought it would be fun to take our three service station dealers to Montreal to see a hockey game and then go to the Playboy Club after. We always interviewed the dealers we selected for the three stations that Phillips had built. They had to give us a deposit and buy a beginning inventory of tires, batteries, accessories and gasoline. We had a few of them go in on a shoestring and not make it. However, most of the time if the guys could pay the deposit on the initial order of gas and TBA (tires, batteries, and accessories) we figured they would probably make out all right and be successful dealers. In 1970 we had three good dealers. Charlie Phelps ran Country Club 66 station, Butch Cote ran Cloverleaf 66, and Larry Lacallaide ran Hilltop 66. The five of us piled into our Plymouth station wagon and headed for Montreal. We got to the Montreal Forum and bought tickets for the hockey game. Montreal was playing Boston which was always a huge rivalry. Montreal had won a number of Stanley Cup's since Boston's last win. It was a great game. We had a wonderful time watching the game, eating hot dogs, and drinking beer. How could we go wrong? After the game we walked over to the Playboy Club. We ate more food, drank many more drinks, and really enjoyed the attention of the Playboy Bunnies. Butch Cote, who had been in Jamaica with me, made sure that everybody heard the story of me sleeping through my date with the Playboy Bunny. It was a great evening and a perfect way to celebrate 1,000,000 gallons sale. That same year, Butch, our dealer, won the service station of the year award from the Vermont Petroleum Association. He received a watch and the trip to Jamaica.

Ray Johnson (Phillips 66), Butch Cote (Cloverleaf 66 dealer), Terry Sousa (Phillips 66), and Dave Mallory

CHAPTER 18

"Fish tremble at the sound of my name."

UNKNOWN

In 1971 we started feeling a lot better about our success. Terry Sousa, our Phillips representative, told us that we had beat the odds and that Phillips had not expected us to succeed. We were one of a very few "scratch jobbers" who had been successful. We were growing and making a little more money so we raised our salaries again to $7200 each and started taking some vacations. Tom called it the year of the passport because he went to the Swiss Alps with Sally, went to Acapulco with Gloria, and Russia with Elinor. I also went to Acapulco, which was another Purolator Filter trip that we won, and I took Ann who became my wife for a few years. While in Acapulco I caught a beautiful Pacific sailfish. It was the highlight of my trip. Tom and I and the girls rented a jeep and drove up into the back country so we could see some of the scenery. We saw some people in the road and stopped to talk with them. We talked to them in English and they talked to us in Spanish! Well, between our bumbling around with the two languages, the Mexican family invited us into their home for a Coke. In those days the only Coke we knew about was the drink! We had a great time with the family, thanked them profusely, and drove back down to our hotel. That was a great trip.

I drove our Plymouth station wagon to Wyoming on a hunting trip, stopping at Niagara Falls, the Badlands, Mount Rushmore, and Yellowstone Park along the way. Coming into Montana from North Dakota I hit a mule deer at night. The deer slipped and fell just as I got there and I hit him with the frame of the car. It didn't do any damage to the car but it killed the deer. I called the Montana Fish and Wildlife Department and told them which road the deer was on and the mile marker. I didn't give my name and just kept driving after the phone call. The next day I drove to Western Montana and up into Yellowstone through the Redgate pass. I stopped at the top of the pass to eat my sandwich and because of the elevation of 11,000 feet got all out of breath just eating my sandwich. I drove down into Yellowstone and spent two days driving around the park. One day I had a black bear walk up to the car and put his paws on the driver side window. That was quite a thrill even with the window rolled up. I thought maybe the bear could smell my sandwiches. Then I drove down to Jackson Hole and met Gordie Jarvis at the airport. We drove down to Pinedale and spent five days deer hunting with Rusty Gooch as our guide. It was a very successful hunt for both of us and a lot of fun. Gordie rode back with me to Vermont. In eastern Wyoming we ran into a strong snowstorm and about 10 o'clock at night we saw a large heard of mule deer crossing the road with the largest buck that we had ever seen. It was much larger than the two that we had shot. We already had our quota so we just watched it cross the road with the herd of does and just walk away.

Tom had a boat which he used to anchor in front of his mother's house on Lake Champlain. In the wintertime Shelburne Bay would freeze over so Tom would take off the buoy and drop the chain from the anchor down to the bottom. In the spring we would have to figure out a way to find the chain and bring it up to the surface. I had a wet-suit and dive tanks so Tom talked me into going down to look for the chain. He wanted to get his boat in the water as soon as he could in the spring, so when I dove in, the water temperature was only in the high 30s. The wet-suit kept me relatively comfortable except for my face. As soon as the water hit my face around my mask my sinuses squeezed up like a grape turning into a raisin. I found the chain, got out of the water as soon as I could, and promised Tom I would never do it again.

Sometimes after work or on weekends we would take the boat out to Juniper Island in the middle of Lake Champlain. Often we would have a party out there. Sometimes we would water ski and often we would throw empty cans in the water and shoot them with a 22 rifle. The island was owned by the Fayette family. Freddie Fayette, the son, was a former classmate of mine and a good friend of both Tom and me. He made Tom the mayor of the island and I was the road commissioner. It was a joke of course because there were no roads on the island and nobody lived there. One time we were water skiing off the beach and had a funny thing happen. We would stand on the beach with a single ski and make about two or three coils of the ski rope on the beach next to the skier. The driver of the boat would go out slowly until the rope got to the two or three coils and then the skier would holler, "Hit it!" Then the driver would open up the power of the boat. This process kept us from getting wet when the water was cool. One time I thought I had two or three coils next to me and told Tom to hit it. However, just as I hollered to him I noticed four more coils next to the two or three that I had rolled up. I hollered, "Hold it," but it was too late. I should have let go of the rope but I didn't. When the rope finally got tight the boat was really flying and very quickly so was I! The ski stayed, but I flew off the beach and went about 10 feet into the water. It was a really funny sight and one that we still laugh about.

One day while I was driving around looking for new business, I noticed a store being built in Milton. I stopped in and talked with Doug. He had retired from General Electric and was building the store to run during his retirement. We talked for quite a while about General Electric and I told him I had worked for three months and never knew what my job was. He said I probably was not the only one with that problem. He was very happy to leave the place and forget about it. This gave us something in common to talk about and we established a relationship. I encouraged him to do business with us, which he agreed. So we sent Tom off to the bank again to put in tanks and pumps. Doug never did a huge amount of gas but the account paid for itself and added to our gasoline total.

In April Phillips came crawling to us and asked us if we would take over the station in St. Albans. The distributor had gone bankrupt and now they had nobody to run the station. We felt really bad for them! We really enjoyed seeing Phillips eat crow. We were happy to take over the station because it meant more sales for us, gave us a chance to win more contests with them, and also gave us the territory which had been ours originally. The store that we had just signed in Milton was actually in this new territory, also.

Would you believe that after we bailed Phillips out by taking over St. Albans they jabbed us in the back again. They signed a new jobber or distributor in Rutland called Midway Oil. Phillips gave Midway the southern portion of Vermont. Our rep, Terry Sousa, gave us the same argument again saying that we hadn't developed the territory and we would get more exposure with the Phillips brand being sold throughout the state. We really didn't feel squeezed by Phillips because we still had a big territory and, as I said before, it was much easier for us to develop customers closer to our warehouse.

Phillips also purchased a piece of land in South Burlington in a prime location with the intention of building a new gasoline station which we would also run. The land sat empty for the rest of the year and we always thought it was rather strange that they didn't start building. We would find out why the following year.

In 1969 we had asked our landlord if we could build a second-story in our warehouse so we could move our office there. This also would allow us to use the upstairs for things like fan belts, ignition parts, light bulbs, and many other accessories that we carried. Bernie agreed, so we hired a laborer to build the second-story for us and we moved in. One summer day we heard there was a rumor going around that our warehouse was going to be robbed that night. At the time, South Burlington didn't have much of a police force and we didn't trust them with the information, so we figured we'd handle the situation ourselves. That night Tom and I hid our vehicles and moved into our warehouse. We brought food, sleeping bags, flashlights and shotguns. We quietly ate our sandwiches, drank our soda, and waited around for it to get dark. We had arranged our sleeping bags upstairs in the loft so that we could see the front door and the overhead door. We decided that every two hours we would change places. One of us would watch the doors and the other one would sleep and then we would rotate. We stayed until after dawn but nobody showed up. We heard another rumor that said the word had gotten out that we were sleeping in the warehouse and apparently that solved the problem because we never got broken into. We think that somebody tipped off the police department and also warned the robbers and told them not to fool around with us. That was fine with us. Apparently shotguns were a nice deterrent.

CHAPTER 19

Question: What do you call a bull the sleeps?

ANSWER: A BULLDOZER!

Late in the summer of 1971 I noticed a building being built in Hardwick. Well, I thought, maybe I can get a new account, so I stopped in, looked around the building, but nobody was there. The building hadn't been completed yet but I noticed a house up the street, so I went and knocked on the door. A woman came to the door and I asked her if she knew who the owner was of the building going up. She said her husband was building it and it was going to be an automotive repair garage. I introduced myself to them and he said his name was Gordon Appleby. I talked with them both for a long time and they weren't sure if they wanted to put in gasoline. I used my same line saying that we were a local company representing Phillips 66 and we could service them much better than the major oil companies. They said they would talk it over and give us a call in a few days. I left feeling a bit down because I hadn't made a sale. Low and behold, three days later they called and Gordon told me to come up because he wanted to talk to me. I drove up to see them and they said they had decided that they would like to put in gasoline with one condition. He said he wasn't planning on paving the yard but he wanted us to supply the gravel and grade it for him. I agreed because I thought we could get it done fairly cheaply. I sent Tom off to the bank again and we got the money for the tanks, the pumps and the gravel. The Chittenden Bank had been very good to us and every time we went in for a loan they gave it to us. However, we had also been very good to them. All of our loans were supposed to be five year loans. We never missed a payment and a number of our loans were already paid off.

The next day I went over to the Pizzagalli warehouse and saw Butch who was in charge of the warehouse and had been very good to us. I told him our problems and he just laughed. He brought me out to the yard, had me climb up on a bulldozer, and showed me how to run it. After about 10 minutes he declared I was good to go. The next day we had the gravel delivered to the garage and again I went to see Butch. He gave me a dump truck with a trailer, pointed out which bulldozer I should take, told me to load it on the trailer, drive it to Hardwick, and start grading the gravel. He lived near the garage and said he would stop by on his way home and finish whatever I didn't have done. I loaded the bulldozer on the trailer, after a few tries, and tied it down with some heavy chains. I drove the truck to Hardwick and unloaded the bulldozer. The gravel was in five or six different piles around the yard. I had no idea where to start or what to do. I thought it would make sense to start with the pile closest to the building and work my way out towards the road. It was a good thing I wasn't being paid by the hour for grading the driveway. I really didn't know whether to push or pull or try to move a lot or a little at a time. After fooling around for an hour or so, I began to get the hang of it and actually started getting something done. I spent about two hours moving the piles around and actually had it fairly smooth when Butch arrived. He looked at the yard and said I had done a decent job, but had graded it sloping toward the building instead of away from it. He spent about half an hour touching up what I had done wrong and when he got done, everything looked great. I loaded the bulldozer back on the trailer and drove it back to the Pizzagalli warehouse. Three days later Walt Myers went up with his crew and installed the tanks and pumps. He had to move around some of the gravel but smoothed it out when he was done. This was another new account close to our tree farm and was pretty much the end of the line for the distance we wanted to travel from our warehouse. It was about 60 miles away and gave me a pretty busy day. I would start at Hilltop 66, go to The Market in Essex Center, on to Ray Lamere's in Morrisville, and finish up at Applebey's in Hardwick. I always called all of the accounts the day before I went so I could deliver any TBA that they might need. Usually I could get everything in our station wagon, but when it didn't fit I would take the Chevy van. Needless to say the accounts right in the Burlington area were able to get their product quicker. They were the biggest accounts we had, so even though they used more, it was easier to get everything to them when they needed it.

When we bought the Chevrolet van, Tom came up with the idea of putting a billboard on the side of the van with interchangeable letters so we could put messages on the billboard as we drove it around town or parked it in the yard of one of our stations to advertise a sale, a new dealer or anything special that was going on - Christmas greetings and so forth. We named the van "Power Pete" and it got to be quite well known in the area. Vermont, as well as South Burlington, had very strict billboard laws; with our movable billboard we were able to get around the laws. The zoning administrator in South Burlington never quite knew how to deal with us so when we had our van parked at a location for more than a few days he would call up to plead with us to move it so he wouldn't get in trouble. It always took us a few days to get it moved and when we did, we usually moved to another location. We kept them hopping, but everything worked out fine.

CHAPTER 20

"Don't talk unless you can improve on the silence."

VERMONT PROVERB

Although we didn't know it at the beginning of the year, 1972 turned out to be a year of transition. Our Phillips business was going well so we raised our salaries again to $7800 apiece. We were having fun selling Christmas trees, Vexar cones, and gasoline. Life was great!

Politically, Vermont had been a Republican state until Phil Hoff was elected governor in 1960. From that time on it became difficult for a Republican to win office. Jim Douglas, a Republican, who would eventually become the state treasurer and later the Vermont governor, was elected to the Vermont House of Representatives from his hometown. Our good friend Fred Hackett, one of the original owners of Power Petroleum, decided to run for governor. We supported him with time and money and he beat Jim Jeffords in the primary. Jim would later become the lone Vermont representative in Washington. Fred was running against Tom Salmon for the governor's office. We went to the winners' party in Montpelier thinking that Fred, who was favored, would win easily. We were wrong. The party turned out to be a bust as the returns came in and Fred lost. That was one of my only times I was involved in politics. The only other time was to help my father become an alderman in Burlington. Fred went on to be an advisor to many Vermont politicians, both Republican and Democrat.

Tom and I learned our lesson on politics that year; we also learned our lesson on "hot tips" in the stock market. Jim Fayette was highly involved in a company called Thermal Wire. They were supposed to be an up-and-coming manufacturer of high-tech wire. We both invested in the "sure thing" company. After three years of no return, the company went bust. So much for "hot tips." Jimmy had another one a few years later. It was a cure for cancer based on orange peelings. We passed on that one.

Our social lives were entertaining. We didn't just work. Tom had built the "Mad Pad" as he liked to call it, at Pine Haven Shore. It was across the road from his mother's house. When Peggy married a wonderful retired IBM engineer, Tom moved out. I spent many happy days there with him after water skiing or going out to dinner or playing cards. Our trips to Juniper Island were frequent and every Fourth of July we would put on a fireworks display that my parents would watch from Burlington. We bought the fireworks at "South of the Border", a tourist trap on the border of North and South Carolina, on our many trips to or from Florida.

I love to hunt and fish so I went hunting for bobcat in Stratton, Maine. The first day I went out with my guide it was 55° below zero! Even the bobcats were smart enough to stay in their den. As the week went on, every day was a little warmer and by the end of the week the dogs were able to tree a bobcat.

Tom had been dating a few women but had not found the right one yet. I introduced him to a friend, Elinor Murphy. I was going out with Ann Brown and they had a mutual friend who wanted to have a fondue party. Carolyn said, "Bring an unusual meat," knowing that I liked to hunt. Since I never shot anything that I wouldn't eat, I had bobcat meat at home which is what I brought to the party. Ann and I were the only ones who knew what the meat was; we told everybody what it was after the party. Tom got very sick after the party, but I think it was the many glasses of wine rather than the meat that made him sick. The fondue dinners were a lot of fun and we continued to do them. Over the years we have cooked elk, caribou, black buck, water buffalo, Pere David, mountain lion, antelope, moose, bear, five kinds of deer, alligator, sheep, and goats. We always vote after the meal to see which meat was the favorite out of the four or five kinds that we usually have. Two different women voted for the mountain lion and a number of people loved the antelope.

Tom and I were always quite generous with our time and we each allowed the other partner time off to go on vacations. Tom loved to go to Europe, sometimes to ski and I loved to go hunting and fishing. We were always able to accommodate each other. One time when Tom was on vacation, Power Petroleum ran out of money. We had more loads of gasoline to pay for then we had money to cover them. During the last few years that we were in business a load of 7500 gallons of gasoline was costing us about $2200. Today, a load of gasoline would cost about $26,000! Quite a change in price in 40 years. I was sitting in the office wondering how to pay Phillips; they were pretty sticky on being paid on time. My solution was to send the credit cards and the check one day late and blame the mail. This gave me an extra day to run around to the stations and pick up the credit cards and money. I got Phillips paid and they got their money late but the mail must have held it up. We had a great reputation for paying them and everybody else on time, so they didn't say anything. There were also some weeks when neither of us were able to take our paychecks because there wasn't enough money to cover them. However, we were always able to catch up eventually.

Tom was in demand as a speaker at parties, weddings, and friendly gatherings. He enjoyed making his talks informal and usually biblical. Many times over the years he would begin by saying, "And it Came to Pass..." I had agreed to marry Ann in May of 1972; of course, Tom was my best man. In the toast at the reception Tom gave the best man toast beginning with "And it Came to Pass..." He went on at length and everyone commented on what a great speech it was. Tom and I had again won a Purolator trip and this time it was to Aruba. Tom graciously gave up his trip and said that Ann and I could use the trip as our honeymoon. Aruba is a gorgeous island which we thoroughly enjoyed.

While we were gone, Tom took care of our German Shepherd, "Duffy." When Tom's paperboy came around early in the morning, Duffy decided to follow him on his route. Tom came out of the "Mad Pad" and discovered she was gone. He was in a panic. He called his paperboy and asked him if he knew where the dog was. He said yes, Duffy was in one of two places near Tom's. Tom went up and rescued our dog before we returned from our trip. Good thing for him.

CHAPTER 21

"Chittenden Bank's core value is aimed at sustained growth and balance attained through traditional banking, targeted acquisitions and specialized businesses."

CHITTENDEN BANK BROCHURE

Meanwhile, things were getting interesting at Power Petroleum. Toward the end of 1972, Phillips, in their infinite wisdom, made the decision to leave northern New England. They said they weren't making enough money and wanted to pull back. What a mess for us. We had a warehouse full of TBA, many great customers to supply, two vehicles which neither of us would use as personal vehicles, and we would also be out of a job. We talked to some of the major oil companies in our area about supplying us with product. If you older readers can remember, 1972 was the year of long lines at the gas pumps because of an artificial shortage caused by Congress and the major oil companies. Nobody was interested in us. We were the perfect example of "up the creek without a paddle."

In January of 1973 Phillips gave us a few weeks to liquidate and then they would not sell us anymore gasoline. Ron Prater, who was the Ashland Petroleum sales rep, and his wife had become good friends. We had gone hiking together on the Long Trail in Vermont many times and had completed a large portion of it. Tom and I had purchased a few loads of gasoline from Ron for our unbranded places such as Avis and Pizzagalli because his product was cheaper, so we had established a good credit rating with Ashland. We got caught by Phillips who said we were breaking their contract by buying gasoline from other companies. However, now we didn't care. So in January we started purchasing more product from Ron to build up our credit.

We had purchased many of our automotive parts from Maynard Auto. Gordie Jarvis, who I had gone hunting and fishing with, was our salesman. He very generously took back all of the current inventory of ignition parts, belts, hoses, light bulbs, and other items. We stocked up our dealers with as much Phillips products as they could take and sold what was left at our cost just to get rid of it. Good hearted Phillips would not take back anything.

The one good thing to come out of this was that Phillips came to us and gave us the first option on the three stations they owned, the piece of land in South Burlington, and the lease on Cloverleaf 66 in South Burlington. Off to the bank again. This time it was serious. Phillips said the price was $330,000 for all the properties. That was a lot of money for two young guys who were about to lose their jobs! Tom talked to Hilton Wick, the president of Chittenden Bank, who asked us how much money we were putting in. Tom said, "Nothing." That floored Hilton! Tom said, his voice a little higher, "We still owe you $70,000!" That was what we still owed on our loans for the tanks and pumps at our accounts. Hilton asked what we planned to do with the stations and how we were going to pay the bank. That seemed like a legitimate question. We told him we were going to try to lease the stations to a major oil company. We also told him we still owned a tree farm in North Wolcott and a gas station in South Hero. We could sell one or both and also the piece of land in South Burlington which we would be buying. That impressed Hilton. He said he would have to clear the loan at a board meeting and would let us know whether it passed or not.

Tom and I had to wait almost two weeks for the board meeting and I have to say we were on edge. It was kind of a mixed blessing. If we got the loan, we were facing a huge responsibility and debt, but the potential for a big payoff went with the stations. If we didn't get the loan, Power Pete was dead and we had nothing to show for five years of hard work, but we wouldn't have any debt. Interesting problems.

The board meeting went well, that is to say, our loan was approved with one caveat. Our parents had to sign the loan also. We had built ourselves an excellent reputation for paying our bills but we were both young and the bank felt our parents would add some stability and insurance for them. Our parents, somewhat reluctantly, signed off on the loan with us. Hilton said the Chittenden didn't have enough money to give us so they went to the Burlington Savings Bank and the two banks each supplied half the money for our loan.

Now we were under pressure. We had $330,000 lined up; the interest alone at 9% for 15 years was $3341.25 per month! We told Phillips that we would buy the stations. The banks set a date for the closing, but said money was tight and there was a chance they might not have enough money on the day of the closing. Tom was astounded and dismayed. He consulted with a close friend who was a bank director and successful businessman. His friend said that was possible with the tight money supply but to call him if the bank could not do the closing. He said he would transfer sufficient funds to our bank so the closing could take place. A huge weight was lifted from our shoulders. It was a wonderful lesson in friendship and being there when needed. Tom and I both hope we have been that kind of friend through life. Happily, the bank was able to close on our loan without the transfer. All of a sudden we owned a bunch of property with basically no supplier. Boy did we have our necks out. This is where Ron Prater and Ashland came to our rescue. Phillips cut off our supply and Ron started selling all of our gas to us. The gas shortage was still on and all the companies had a quota for each month. We exceeded our quota with Ashland in less than two weeks. We also exceeded our credit limit. Ron asked us to pay the invoices early and we might be able to continue for a while but he warned us that Ashland would also shut us down if we continued very long.

In the meantime, we were busy looking for somebody to lease our stations. We asked Mobil, Shell, Chevron, Citgo, Esso, and Texaco. Esso, which later became Exxon, wanted to lease the stations year-by-year. We said no. We wanted a 15 year lease so our loans would be paid off and the stations would be ours free and clear. After many meetings, phone calls, and negotiations, Texaco agreed to take the four stations on a 15 year lease. Cloverleaf 66, which we never owned, had a 15 year lease from Phillips with three five-year options. What a relief! On April 1 (not a joke) of 1973, Tom went to Boston to sign the contract with Texaco. The president of Texaco had been out of the country for a week, so we had to wait for his return before he could sign

off on the contract. We sweated out the three months of owning a lot of property and owing a lot of money with no real way
to pay it back. With the signed Texaco leases, we refinanced
the stations at 7 1/2% with the First of Boston. We paid off the
Chittenden Bank loan and the Texaco rents paid off the First of
Boston. We had purchased all of the property with no money out
of our pockets. We really were learning the "smart guy" thing.
We paid the interest for the three months and had a big party
when Tom returned from Boston. Power Petroleum was effec-
tively out of business.

In 1964 a movie called *Zorba the Greek* came out. It was the
story of two guys who put everything they had into a business.
They constructed a log chute down the side of a mountain to
get the logs down to the river below. After working furiously to
get the chute done they loaded the first logs on the chute and
sent them on their way. About two thirds of the way down the
mountain the chute collapsed and they lost everything. Zorba
said to his partner, as they were watching everything from the
riverbank, "Let's dance." They danced away on the riverbank
until they were exhausted and then went and got drunk. Tom
and I thought the movie was a perfect scenario for us. We had
invested money and time into Power Petroleum and had the
potential for losing everything just like Zorba and his partner; but
the difference was, we were successful!

CHAPTER 22

"In 1958, Angelo G. Pizzagalli and two of his sons,
Angelo and Remo, founded Pizzagalli Pre-cast Stone to
handle masonry construction and manufacture cut stone."

PIZZAGALLI CONSTRUCTION BROCHURE

W e felt that we had been good to all our customers. Interstate 66 in St. Albans, Hilltop 66 in Winooski, Cloverleaf 66 in South Burlington, and Country Club 66 in Burlington were no longer Phillips. They were flying the Texaco sign and were selling Texaco products. Island Service Center in South Hero was also branded Texaco. We sold Pizzagalli and Avis, along with the rest of our customers, to Champlain Oil, who carried the Citgo brand. I would eventually go to work for them. Everybody was taken care of and now we had to find jobs and try to sell some properties to pay our bills at the bank.

I interviewed for a job at Noyes Tire, a company based in Maine with 15 stores throughout Maine, New Hampshire, and Vermont. They were looking for a salesman to introduce Michelin truck and off-road tires in Vermont. I was their man.

Tom went to work for Pizzagalli Construction. Angelo, the president, wanted Tom to work in the real estate division, but Tom said no thanks, I'm retired. He would be content to work in the warehouse and drive trucks. He wouldn't have to do any thinking after the whole Power Petroleum closing. So we both had jobs and now in our spare time we had to figure out what to do with all of our real estate.

We were property managers, owning four gasoline stations, a piece of bare land, a tree farm, and the lease on a fifth station. Our first thought was to sell the piece of land in South Burlington. It was just sitting there and not producing any income. We heard the owner of VIP Gasoline stations wanted to expand into Vermont. Bob Spain had several locations in New York and was looking for land in Vermont to build a station. We met with him and he really liked the location. He said he would take it so we were happy because we thought it was sold. Wrong! He said he was married to Christine McGuire, one of the popular McGuire sisters of the 50s and 60s. He also told us that Christine's sister Phyllis was very involved with Sam Giancona, a well-known mafia boss. Bob laughed when we asked him about the mafia and he said he would get back to us shortly but we never heard from him again. We later found out that he was involved in a messy divorce and went out of business. We never knew if the mafia had anything to do with it or not.

Back to square one. Ernie Ross was our dealer in South Hero, Vermont at Island Service Center. He said he wanted to buy the station from us. Ernie was a Southern boy from Tennessee and you really had to like the guy. As I said before, he was a hard worker and made friends with everybody. He went to the bank and borrowed as much as he could and we financed the rest. Every so often, he would get behind in his payments, and would disappear to Tennessee for a few days. When he came back he would catch up on his payments. Tom and I always thought that he had a stash of money in Tennessee and he would bring enough back to make his payments for a while. He ran the station for a few years, had a gift shop, sold insurance, bought a gravel quarry and eventually went belly up on all of his businesses. In all fairness to him, he continued to pay us every month for many years until he went back to Tennessee. He never quite paid us off but he did pretty well and didn't owe us too much at the end. I talked to him just before he died about his stash of money in Tennessee. He laughed and said it was a myth, that there really never was a stash of money there. Since he had nothing to lose at that point I believed him.

In June of 1973 we heard that Reilly Tire in Rutland wanted to expand to the Burlington area. Ray Reilly Junior came to see us and wanted to take a look at the land we had for sale in South

Burlington. We went there and measured it; he thought it would work well for him. We fought for a long time on the price, but we held firm. I had mixed feelings about selling the land to them. Of course I wanted to sell the land so we could pay the bank, but Reilly Tire was a major competitor of Noyes Tire where I worked. In the end, selling the land was more important. We finally did make a deal with Ray and he formed a new Corporation with his father, Dick Eastman and himself. They were a thorn in my side the whole five years I worked for Noyes. However, now Tom and I could finish paying off the bank for all the of the equipment loans left from Power Petroleum, have some money left over, and collect the money from Texaco for the next 15 years. Life was good.

Part III

The Later Years

CHAPTER 23

*"Calvin Coolidge was the greatest man who
ever came out of Plymouth Corner, Vermont."*

CLARENCE DARROW

The transition from owners to worker bees took a while for us, but was a pleasant change. We no longer had to worry about paying the company bills, irate customers, wondering if we had enough money to get paid, and keeping the bank happy. We could easily sell enough timber and Christmas trees to pay the bills at our tree farm and the Texaco leases paid for the gas stations, as well as the taxes and insurance. My job at Noyes Tire was interesting. Michelin tires were more expensive than any other brand, but their truck tires lasted much longer than the others and could be recapped more often for use on trailers. The off-road tires also lasted much longer and because of the steel belts they did not cut when used in places like quarries. Tom's job at Pizzagalli was fun also. He was driving trucks for them, delivering equipment to the different job sites, and also working in the warehouse. We were both able to go home at night not worrying about company bills or problems, and could get a good night's sleep.

Tom sold his motorboat and bought the Eagle, a beautiful sailboat. He had never sailed before but the former owner's son helped Tom learn how to sail and also learn about the boat. Tom would often get home from work and go sailing in Shelburne Bay. I was settling into married life. We put a wood stove in our Jericho home and often after work I would cut down some trees, chop wood, or work in our garden. We had very heavy clay soil, so I had two truckloads of sand delivered and dumped into the garden. I also dumped all the grass clippings and leaves from the yard, so the garden did very well.

The years were rolling by. The stations and the tree farm were appreciating in value. Peggy and Clyde were living in Palm Beach for the winters and at Pine Haven for the summers. Tom was spending quite a bit of time with a friend named Vernice. She would often come down to Tom's and go sailing with him. She and Tom also went on a trip to China. Rocky Maurais, who I used to shoot against in rifle competitions in school, talked me into joining the 40th Army Band. That got me away from the artillery unit that I was in, and hated. I might not have stayed in the National Guard if it hadn't been for Rocky getting me into the band. He also got me to join the Vermont National Guard Rifle Team which was a lot of fun for many years.

1977 was another year of transition, at least for me. My band and shooting buddy, Rocky, passed away from stomach cancer which was a huge blow to me. Ann decided the grass was greener elsewhere and headed out to pasture. She just didn't believe in the phrase, "until death do you part." She tried the marriage thing three times, I was the middle one, and she failed each time after five years. I guess she decided at that point that she shouldn't be married.

The good thing that happened to me that year was my promotion to First Sergeant of the 40th Army Band. I had mixed emotions on the day I took the job because Rocky would have been the First Sergeant had he lived. I tried my best to do a good job for him. I would have much rather given up the job to have Rocky alive. I held the position for over 24 years, probably a Vermont record.

This was a happy time for Tom. Peggy had deeded her house in Shelburne to him. He continued to live across the street in the "Mad Pad" and rented out the big house. Tom and Vernice continued their travel around the world and also spent a great deal of time sailing on Tom's Eagle. However, in 1979, Vernice was transferred by Pizzagalli to the Turks and Caicos Islands and Tom was transferred to Gainesville, Florida. That was pretty much the end of that relationship.

When Tom was working in Burlington he would often drive a car to Florida for people who wanted their car in Florida but wanted to travel down by plane. Sometimes I would drive down with him to Lake City, FL where we would meet Mom and Dad. Dad had retired in 1978 and he and Mom had purchased a condo in Fort Walton Beach, FL. Tom would continue the drive down to Palm Beach and I would go to Fort Walton Beach with Mom and Dad. I would stay for a few days and then fly back to Jericho. Other times I would fly from Portsmouth, New Hampshire, to Eglin Air Force Base in Fort Walton on a KC 135 tanker. There was a pilot whose parents lived near mine and he would schedule a mission on a weekend that we were free. It was fun because we would refuel fighter jets such as A-10s, F-4s, and F-16s. I would lie on the couch next to the boom operator and watch the planes as they came up to be refueled.

Refueling A-10 from a KC-135 Tanker

During that summer I heard that Champlain Oil was looking for a commercial salesman. I called the owner, Tony Cairns, and talked with him; we decided that would be a good job for me. We knew each other a little bit from my days with Power Petroleum, so it didn't require a long interview. However, again I had somebody training me for the job who really didn't like what he was doing. He wanted to become a retail salesman but he didn't want me to succeed which would make him look bad. He didn't show me much about what I was supposed to do or who the customers were. In spite of that, I learned the job quickly and became friends with many of the customers. I continued doing the job for the next 24 years until I retired. Eventually Darryl had the distinction of being the only employee ever fired by Tony in all the years I worked there.

Tom and I continued to treat each other for our birthday dinners every year. Since we weren't always around the Burlington area, we started branching out from Bove's Restaurant. Some of the places we went to were The Summer House in Fort Walton Beach, Florida and the Waterworks in Winooski, Vermont. We were really getting around!

Things were going well for me also. I had a number of friends rent a room from me while going through a divorce or other transition periods in their lives. I had fun with some of them, riding dirt bikes, hunting or fishing. A group of us in the 40th Army Band formed a German Band and we really enjoyed playing at events such as Oktoberfest and various conventions. The 40th Army Band also had many very good rifle marksmen and we won a national award called the Pershing Award, for the unit with the highest percentage of expert marksmen in the country. Pete Young and I were sent to Las Vegas to receive the award for the band. The band also won the Vermont Adjutant General's Rifle Match a number of times, plus a number of national awards with .22 rifles and air guns. The Adjutant General was so proud of us he called us his "shoot and toot" band! I also played Taps at President Coolidge's grave on the Fourth of July which was the anniversary of his birthday. I did that for 22 years; in the beginning I would have lunch after the ceremony with John Coolidge, the president's son.

Playing TAPS at grave of President Coolidge on July 4

The 40th Army Band was also chosen to lead the eight-hour Alpini Festival Parade in Vincenzo, Italy. It was a parade for all the mountain troops in Europe. It was observed by the Italian president and we had to stop in front of his reviewing stand and honor him. We also played a number of concerts throughout northern Italy. The Italian people could not do enough for us. It was a wonderful experience. The band was also sent to Panama for two weeks to do Change of Command Ceremonies, as well as a Pass in Review and retirement ceremonies. While we were there we had a chance to tour the country and also observe many ships going through the Panama Canal.

CHAPTER 24

"Caribou are wild; if they are
domesticated they are called reindeer."

ORACLE EDUCATION FOUNDATION

est any of you readers think all we did was travel and play, you were wrong; well, mostly wrong. Along with our jobs, we still had real estate to manage. We were thinking that if the right deal came along we would sell any or all of the stations, plus the tree farm. We thought it would be nice to have some money to invest for our retirement. In 1981, our first deal came along. Gordie Jarvis, our former supplier of auto parts, fishing, and hunting friend, approached us about buying Hilltop in Winooski. Gordie knew the dealer was leaving the station. Further, he knew Texaco wanted to stop directly running the station and were looking for a distributor to take it over. Gordie already ran two other Texaco stations in the Burlington area and thought this would also be a good one for him. He offered Gary, the dealer, full price for his inventory. Walter Simendinger also really wanted the station and had approached us about buying it; however, he was not willing to pay anywhere near what it was worth. He also approached Gary about taking over the station but did not want to pay him anything for his inventory. We found out through the years that this was one of Walter's tactics. Sometimes he got what he wanted for nothing and sometimes he did not. He did not succeed with us. It was an easy choice for Gary. He told Gordie to make a deal with us on the station and keep Simendinger out. After two meetings we made a deal with Gordie with one caveat. Gordie had to pay for my hunting trip with him to Newfoundland for caribou, moose, and bear and give Tom a check for the equivalent amount. Gordie bought the station, Gary moved out, and Simendinger steamed. He approached Gordie and said he was a Texaco distributor and that he would supply Gordie with gasoline; however he really wanted the station. Gordie agreed and leased it to him for five years with an option to buy. Gordie never set foot in the station, but all parties were happy. Tom and I invested the money, and Gordie and I had a very successful Newfoundland hunting trip.

One of the benefits of being in the National Guard was free air travel. The VT Air National Guard had a mission to Elmendorf Air Force Base in Alaska. I found out they had room on the plane and I could go. Steve Nicholas and I flew with them to Minot Air Force Base and stayed overnight. While we were there we were watching TV and the announcer came on with a bulletin saying that the Pope had been shot! Steve turned to me and said, "Why would anybody shoot the Pope when Howard Cosell is still alive?" I guess Steve didn't care much for Howard Cosell. The next morning we flew to Alaska and spent ten days fishing and touring. We caught many Halibut and Dolly Varden trout which we cleaned and packed in ice. We filled up a big wooden crate the air guard gave us and were able to bring all our fish home. Alaska is a gorgeous state and it was fun to have a free trip. I promised myself I would go back again.

Not everything that happened was good that year. Tom had a group of friends on his sailboat, the Eagle, maybe a few too many; too many of them moved to one side resulting in the boat capsizing. Fortunately, they weren't too far from land and there were other boats around, so all survived. The boat was later brought up by divers from the bottom of Shelburne Bay, fixed up, and used again by Tom. The good thing was that insurance paid for everything, but it was a scary experience for Tom.

CHAPTER 25

Lake Champlain is the sixth largest freshwater lake in the United States. It is 120 miles long and just over 10 miles wide at its widest point. The lake has a maximum depth of just under 400 feet.

My Champlain Oil territory brought me to the station we owned in St. Albans. I had met the dealer there in 1980, Joe St. Pierre, on a hunting trip, organized by Gordie, to Anticosti Island in Quebec. As it turned out, Joe and I ended up hunting together, so we had quite a bit of time to talk about business and the station. Joe expressed an interest in buying the station. When we got back, I talked with Tom about selling another property and we agreed, as usual, that if the price was right we would sell the station; again to invest the money for retirement. A few months went by and every so often I would stop in to see Joe. Sometimes we would talk about the stations and sometimes we would talk about hunting and fishing. Joe had gotten into fishing for trout and salmon in Lake Ontario and also Lake Champlain. He had stopped doing auto repair in one of the repair bays and started selling fishing tackle in the office and also in the bay. My job at Champlain Oil kept me in touch as I tried to sell him antifreeze and other products. He couldn't buy gasoline from me because of his contract with Texaco. Finally, one day he said he was ready to buy the station. Tom, Joe, and I met and agreed on a price. Joe had his lawyer draw up the papers and we closed on the station. Joe ended up building a second story for his office and another building next door for automobile repairs. He also operated six tow trucks from his location. He ended up going with Gordie and me to

Newfoundland where we teamed up for a bear. We each shot a caribou and a moose.

Tom, who loves to travel, was also having fun. During this time period he made trips to China, Hong Kong, Mexico, and Europe. He had close friends in Vermont with strong ties to Switzerland and enjoyed numerous trips with members of the family to places such as Lugano, Switzerland; Mallorca, Spain, and other interesting places in Europe.

At that time I was dating a wonderful girl from Minnesota, who would eventually become my wife. We heard about a New Hampshire National Guard incentive flight to Hawaii. Pauline was a Captain with the MP's and I was still the First Sergeant in the band. The plane was a KC 135 tanker and we were supposed to refuel fighter jets on the way to Hawaii. Steve Nicholas said he wanted to go with us, so the three of us drove to Portsmouth, New Hampshire and boarded the plane. Shortly after takeoff we lost one of the four engines, so we had to dump some fuel over the ocean because we were too heavy to land, and went back to Portsmouth landing with three engines. The mechanics replaced the engine in about 3 ½ hours and we took off again. However, we were too late for our refueling mission, so we flew directly to Salt Lake City to drop off the people who were going skiing. The next morning we flew to Honolulu. Steve and I checked in to our hotel and smuggled Pauline in with us. We were there for that night, all of the next day and night, and then flew back to Portsmouth. During the one whole day that we were there we took a plane ride to the four main islands of Hawaii. It was a whirlwind trip, but we saw many of the highlights of Hawaii and promised ourselves that we would try to get back there again someday.

Pauline and Dave

Tom and I were on a roll! We still had a tree farm, the Burlington gas station, and we controlled the lease on the station in South Burlington. We weren't trying to sell anything but if you don't have to sell, things just seem to happen. Tom was still working for Pizzagalli in 1983 and one of the foremen was building the Burlington wood chip plant. Because he would be in the warehouse almost every day he would often see Tom. Lucian Gravel lived in Morrisville near our tree farm. I knew Lucian because I used to shoot against him when he was on the Morrisville National Guard Rifle Team. He told Tom that he might be interested in buying our tree farm. We still worked the farm on weekends and I would often go to the farm to do timber stand improvement or to mark the boundaries. One day when I was marking the boundary, I discovered a bear had been following me! I saw his tracks on top of mine when I started back to the car. I never saw the bear and I was just as glad.

Lucian and Tom haggled back and forth for a few months and finally agreed on a price. Tom called me and said we had sold the tree farm. We had the closing in Hyde Park and I told Lucian that I would only sign the papers if I could cut my Christmas tree every year on the farm. He thought that would be just fine. Pauline and I would take our Golden retriever, Kelly, to the farm every year and cut our tree until I retired in 2002. Lucian and Portia built a beautiful home on the property which burned down about 12 years later, but they rebuilt the home and still live there.

Tom had a little mishap that year driving one of the Pizzagalli trucks. He was delivering a bulldozer to one of the job sites and as he was rounding a corner, the bulldozer fell off. In all fairness to Tom, he had not loaded the bulldozer on the trailer, so it wasn't his fault. The owner of the bulldozer, not Pizzagalli, had loaded and secured it. Tom said he would like to secure it differently but the owner said it was fine. I guess he was wrong! I came along just after the accident but there really wasn't much I could do. The bulldozer wasn't damaged and they were able to load it back on the trailer and deliver it. We had many good laughs over the incident, after it was all taken care of.

CHAPTER 26

The Concorde was a turbojet supersonic
passenger airliner. It flew for 27 years.

As 1984 began, Big Brother of George Orwell fame, wasn't watching. We didn't know it in January but we were going to have an eventful year. In May, Pauline and I decided to get married. We had both been married before, learned from our mistakes, and knew what we were looking for. Tom had purchased a replica of his 1955 Ford Thunderbird and he brought me to the church in his car. We had a wonderful celebration with Richard Crocker doing the service and Tom again doing another "And It Came to Pass" speech. A great time was had by all. The reception was held at a friend's home in Grand Isle. After the reception when most of the people had left, Pauline ate the fruit at the bottom of the champagne punchbowl. The fruit had collected a lot of champagne and Pauline was feeling very happy. We had planned to go out for a wonderful intimate dinner that night, but she didn't quite feel up to it. Instead we went to Joe's Snack Bar for dinner. We continued the tradition of having an anniversary dinner at Joe's until we moved to Florida. Two years after we were married in the Congregational Church, we were married in the Catholic Church. Over the years we have renewed our marriage vows on three different cruises throughout the world.

And it came to pass that the one known as Pauline did enter the house of David seeking to interest he that is known as Bruce in policies of insurance. David did note the comeliness of this purveyor of prestigious policies and paused to reflect on his current policy — of celibacy. And so it was that he did pursue this Pauline, the policy purveyor and in time they came to know that they shared many common interests — the joy of fishing, XC skiing, gardening and water beds. Yea truly they did find satisfaction together in music, military pursuits and tickling feet. (It is yet to be determined who is the tickler and the ticklee. And from these interests did spring a love and respect for one another that evidences itself today as they enter the bond of matrimony. (For those of you having trouble following it means they got married) and the call went forth that a wedding feast should be held. Yea I say unto you that the beasts were slaughtered, crops were harvested, and the juice of the grape flowed unceasingly.

And so it is that as we share the joy of this moment with Pauline and David, those of you still able, please rise and join me in wishing these two that the joy and love in your hearts today will grow and multiply over a happy & blessed future.

"And it Came to Pass" speech

Tom giving the speech

Tom celebrated his 50th birthday that July. He and I were still doing our birthday dinners every year at various restaurants and Tom suggested going to London for his dinner. We planned to fly over after work on Friday, tour on Saturday, have the birthday dinner that evening, and fly back to Burlington on Sunday. We wanted to fly at least one way on the Concorde, but it cost as much for one person to fly one way as it did for both of us to fly round-trip. We made our reservations, but when we got to the Burlington Airport, People's Express had canceled our flight to Newark. What to do! Tom called Frank Donahue at Pizzagalli on the off chance a friend of his might be flying somewhere near New York City that night. They were! They had a flight going to White Plains, so we hopped on their little plane and they dropped us off at Newark. We arrived in time to catch our flight to London. How lucky can we be? We had a great birthday dinner for Tom, saw quite a few of the sites in London, and were back to work on Monday morning, tired but happy.

Dave and Tom in London for Tom's 50th birthday

50th birthday dinner

In August Pauline and I went on our honeymoon. We flew to Seattle and rented a car; we took the ferry to Butchart Gardens in Victoria, British Columbia, and drove to Mount Rainier, Mount St. Helen's, Mount Hood, through the redwoods in California, and ended up with a Mallory family reunion in California where many of my cousins and my uncle lived. We talked about the trip with my parents because we had seen Dad's brother. After talking so much about the trip, we decided to do the trip with them in two years. Again we had a wonderful time and we were amazed at the change in Mount St Helen's, which had blown up a few years before we went out on our honeymoon.

That winter Tom bought a new Cadillac for his mother. I decided to ride to Florida with him. He dropped me off at my parents in Fort Walton Beach and went on to Palm Beach to deliver the car to his mother. It was a wonderful Christmas present for her.

CHAPTER 27

S unset Celebration is a nightly arts festival at Mallory Square Dock in Key West, Florida. The participants of this Key West attraction consist of arts and crafts exhibitors, street performers, food carts, psychics and of course the thousands of tourists from around the world who visit the Key West Art show. Each night around two hours before sunset masses of people, both local and tourists alike, flock to the water's edge to experience a multicultural happening and to watch the sun sink into the Gulf of Mexico.

Sunset at Mallory Square

Dave, Pauline and Tom at Key West

Tom had been " working" in construction for 12 years, but was starting to feel as if he should do something about his mother and Clyde. They were getting old but were still living in their home in Palm Beach and needed some help. They were not willing to move into any kind of retirement home, so Tom, being conscious of what was happening to them, retired on Labor Day in 1985 at the age of 51. We had both invested wisely and our investments were doing quite nicely, so he felt he could live with them and let them live out their days at home. Peggy and Clyde had come to Vermont for the summer for the last time, so we celebrated Tom's birthday with my parents, Peggy and Clyde, Pauline, Tom and me at the Waterworks restaurant in Winooski. Tom moved to Florida and rented the property he had in Vermont. We would have to be more creative now about our birthday dinners.

In 1987 our 15-year lease with Texaco ran out. We needed to find somebody to take over Cloverleaf in South Burlington and

Country Club in Burlington. Since I was working for an oil company at the time, it seemed like a good place to start. Bingo! Tony Cairns owned Champlain Oil Company where I worked and was dying to get our South Burlington station. There was a rather complicated series of six leases starting with the landowner, the builder, Phillips, Power Petroleum, Texaco and finally the dealer running the station. Tony went to all the parties, bought the property and all the leases except ours. We had a five-year option which we kept. That location was all set until 1992. Tom and I continued to get a check for that location every month for the next five years. Tony also said he would supply the station in Burlington. Champlain Oil had a dealer, Armand Kaigle, down the street from our station and he was very busy. He felt he could use our place for his extra work and sell gasoline there also. Great! We were all set again.

My birthday dinners were held in Florida for the next few years. One year we celebrated in Key West at a restaurant called the Hot Tin Roof on Duval Street overlooking Mallory Square. Where else? The next year we all went to the Flamingo Resort in the Everglades and celebrated my birthday there. That resort was later destroyed by hurricanes Katrina and Wilma.

Tom was able to get to Vermont for his birthdays, so we went to Cafe Shelburne in Shelburne or Ho Ho's in Essex. We were enjoying many great restaurants for our birthdays. Some years Pauline and I would meet Tom in Ft. Walton and we would celebrate both birthdays at different places with my parents. We loved the Chop Shop for their steaks and also the Magnolia Grill. One year we celebrated Tom's birthday at Eglin Air Force Base. We had to be creative because Tom had become a resident of Florida to get away from Vermont taxes and he really couldn't stay away very long from his parents. He felt he needed to spend most of his time with them, especially during hurricane season.

Dad Mallory, Dave, Mom Mallory, Tom and Pauline at the Chop House in Fort Walton Beach

Dave, Mom Mallory, Pauline, Dad Mallory, Tom at Eglin Air Force Base

In 1992 I celebrated my 50th birthday. Tom felt he could get away for a week or so and have somebody stay with his parents. He asked me where I wanted to go for my birthday and I suggested Cozumel so we could snorkel and Las Vegas so we could see some shows and tour the area. So off we went. Cozumel was our first stop and the snorkeling was fantastic. I had my birthday dinner at Ponchos Backyard. The margaritas were wonderful and Tom said the food was great also. I don't remember. After we finished dinner, an entertainer came in who played the pan flute. I always enjoyed listening to the pan flute, so we decided to stay for a few songs. His third song was the theme from *Zorba the Greek* - our song! We felt really weird and special. That is not a normal piece to play on a pan flute, especially in Mexico. In Las Vegas we went to three different shows, gambled, and toured the area. We went to Hoover Dam, which was very impressive. Because Pauline told us to go without her, I decided to buy a thank you gift. I decided on some emerald earrings and pendant. Tom, very generously, suggested that we take the money for Pauline's gift out of our income from the stations. Pauline was very happy with her gift and thanked us both many times.

Tom and Dave in Cozumel after hearing "our" song

CHAPTER 28

*In winter moose eat shrubs and pine cones, but they also
scrape snow with their large hooves to clear areas for
browsing on mosses and lichens.*

VERMONT HUNTING GUIDE

The last two events of our real estate business occurred in 1992.
Armand Kaigle, his son and daughter came to me with an
offer to buy Country Club from us. It wasn't doing a lot of gas
but it was working out well for their repair business. We debated
back and forth and came up with a price we all agreed on. I
talked with Tom and he agreed with me. I talked with Tony and
he agreed to supply the station with gasoline. Everything went
very smoothly and we sold off our last piece of property. Armand
ran one station and Ray, his son, ran our place. They ran them
both for many years until Armand retired. Ray eventually sold our
station to some very enterprising people and they completely
redid the building and turned it into a restaurant called The Spot.
Tom and I had a delightful lunch there in 2010. Later that year
our lease ran out with Champlain Oil. Tony was happy to stop
giving me a check for the lease every month and actually, it was
nice to have all of our business properties gone. It was the end of
our business, but certainly not the end of our friendship.

In 1994 I was lucky enough to draw one of only fifty moose
permits for Vermont. There were almost 11,000 applications so I
was in a very privileged group. It was a three-day season and I
hunted with a friend, Glenn Brown. We scouted the area for three
weekends and felt confident after seeing some moose while we
were scouting. We hunted hard for the first two days when the
season opened; finally we saw a nice bull and shot it on the third
day. It weighed 757 pounds with antlers that measured 50 inches

across. The fun was over after it fell to the ground. It took 11 of us with trucks and winches three hours to get him out of the woods and onto a trailer so we could bring it home. Unfortunately the meat was very tough but we ate it all.

Tom was still helping Peggy and Clyde. He sold some of Peggy's investments to pay the taxes on their home in Palm Beach which were $13,000. She got mad at Tom and asked, "Don't you have any stock?" Tom answered, "Yes, but it is your house." Peggy replied, "I was saving that money for when I'm old. I want you to buy some 30 year treasuries for me." She was 95 at the time! In 1996 Clyde passed away, followed by Peggy a year later. In 1993 Tom had purchased a condo in Lake Worth and shortly after Peggy and Clyde both passed away, he sold the house in Palm Beach and moved into his condo.

My mother and father moved out of their condo which we had purchased from them in 1992, and moved into Westwood Retirement Home. It was great for them there and they really enjoyed the companionship and all of the activities.

In 1997 I was named by Governor Howard Dean to the Vermont Fish and Wildlife Board for a period of six years. After two years, I was named chairman, a position I held until the end of my term in 2002.

Pauline, Dave, Tom and Carol Caldwell at Disney dinner

Our birthday dinners continued at the Swan at Disney World for me and at Mona's in Burlington for Tom. In 1999 Pauline, Tom and I went to Alaska for 12 days. We celebrated Tom's birthday in Anchorage at Sullivan's Steakhouse. Later that year I bought out Tom's interest in our business. We still had income from the mortgage we held on the tree farm; also a few people still owed us money which we would get once in a while. We never did get it all. By selling his share to me, Tom, who was a resident of Florida, wouldn't have to pay the exorbitant Vermont income taxes. With all that money coming in, Tom was able to take a 127 day around the world cruise. It was a great educational trip and one which he often talks about. Unfortunately, not too many years later the company went bankrupt.

In 2000 Pauline's father passed away. My dad passed away in 2001 and my mom in 2002.

CHAPTER 29

The ice hotel near Quebec City is built each December for an early January opening. It has a four-month lifespan and comes down in April. It usually has about 80 beds, all made of ice but lined with deer furs and covered with mattresses and Arctic sleeping bags. Only the bathrooms are heated and are situated in another area.

QUEBEC TOUR GUIDE

Tom and I continued to travel, sometimes together and sometimes not. Tom went to China, Manila, Hawaii and many other spots around the world. Pauline and I went to a different Caribbean island every year during her school vacations. We also went to Hawaii, on a Baltic cruise to seven countries, a driving vacation to five European countries, and just recently, on a cruise to Iceland and the Arctic Ice Cap. We also spent six nights in Quebec City; one of the nights we slept in the Ice Hotel, a very unique experience. While there we did some cross-country skiing, hiking, snowmobiling, and were able to drive our own dog sled for a couple of hours. It was a great trip.

Pauline and Dave in a "sitting room" at the Ice Hotel in Quebec

Tom and I went to China and Tibet to celebrate his 70th birthday. Tibet is the only place I have ever been where the sidewalk vendors sold oxygen bottles because the elevation was always over 12,000 feet and went up to 15,000 feet.

Dave and Tom at the Great Wall of China

**Potala Palace in Lhasa Tibet. Home of the
Dalai Lama when he is allowed to come back.**

Pauline and I retired from our jobs in 2002 and moved to Florida. I got my real estate license and Pauline taught for a few years, and in recent years did some substitute teaching and tutoring. I joined two honor guard groups which allows me to play Taps a few times a week at Bay Pines National Cemetery. We all continue to travel and eat. Recently, two of our favorite places to celebrate birthdays and other occasions have been The Black Pearl Restaurant in Dunedin, FL and Phillips Point Club in Palm Beach, FL.

I try to play golf every week (some people would hardly call it golf) and try to fish at least once a week. Pauline says I get grumpy if I don't fish at least once a week!

Have we been lucky? You bet we have. However, we made some good business decisions and prayed a lot. God was very good to us and immensely blessed us.

I couldn't have asked for a better person to do business with and a better wife to support our requests. That is our story. The American Dream is still alive and we are living proof. We hope you enjoyed our tale and we hope you can be as successful and as happy as we are.

Dave Mallory was born in Burlington, VT in 1942. He enjoyed many years of hunting, fishing, golfing, traveling and enjoying wonderful relationships with many friends. Dave is a member of the Clearwater Community Band and the Second Time Arounders Marching Band and does real estate for Free Realty. He now lives in Seminole, FL with his wonderful wife, Pauline.

Tom Marx was born in 1934 in Long Island, NY. He grew up in VT where he enjoyed skiing, hiking and boating. He has traveled extensively including two trips around the world, one in the northern hemisphere and one in the southern hemisphere. He feels his life has been very blessed in so many ways. A perfect example is having Dave Mallory as an outstanding business partner and lifelong friend. Tom has lived in FL since 1985.